Yikes! I HAVE TO TALK IN CHURCH

How to Prepare and Deliver a Great Sacrament Meeting Talk

Bill Mansell

I0809108

M!NDPERK

Sandy, Utah

Published by: MindPerk, Inc.,
2133 East 9400 South #129
Sandy, UT 84093

Distributed by: Brigham Distribution
110 South 800 West
Brigham City, UT 84302-2400
(435) 723-6611

This work is not an official publication of The Church of Jesus Christ of Latter-day Saints. The views expressed herein are the responsibility of the author and do not necessarily represent the position of the Church.

ISBN 978-0-9836540-0-1

Library of Congress Control Number: 2011931934

www.SpeakingInChurch.com

This book is dedicated,
with deepest affection and love,
to my wife, Marquette,
who has blessed my life
in every way imaginable and
who truly has the gift of speech.

Acknowledgements

I'd like to thank all those who contributed to the success of this book. No one lives in a vacuum, so although I believe the ideas and suggestions in the book to be my own, they are undoubtedly influenced by those who have nurtured and taught me throughout my life. In addition, as I prepared the manuscript, I have felt many times the inspiration of heaven, for which I am truly grateful.

No book is written without the support of dozens of people. I'd like to offer special thanks:

To my wife, Marquette, who read through every chapter and showered me with ideas and support.

To Dian Thomas, whose encouragement, energy, and expertise made the book possible.

To Russ Wood, Daryl Hoole, and Micah Miller, for giving generously of their time to read the manuscript and provide helpful suggestions.

To Tristi Pinkston, my editor, and Richard Haight, my graphic artist, who made this project their own by transforming my rough manuscript into a user-friendly book.

To Annie Oswald, for planting and nurturing the seed that resulted in this book.

To Mark Benson, my mentor, who first taught me how to effectively speak in public, and to dozens of other professional trainers from whom I have learned the finer points of speaking over the years. Truly I stand on the shoulders of giants.

And to my parents, Bill & Annette, for their unwavering support and belief in me.

Contents

Introduction
Why Read This Book

After forty years, I still vividly remember standing in a line of children stretching up to the pulpit, waiting to give my two-line part in a Primary program. I remember my hands sweating, my heart beating fast, and my eyes darting around, looking for any way to escape. My part was written on a small strip of paper which I kept pulling out of my pocket to read and re-read. I remember the panic building inside my chest as the line got shorter and shorter.

As I reached the pulpit, a Primary teacher whispered, "You're next." At that moment, my blood froze, cutting off all oxygen to my brain. (This is not an official medical diagnosis, but it aptly describes what I felt at the time.) I stepped up on the little stool and stared out into the congregation with a feeling of abject terror. I couldn't remember my own name, let alone remember my lines. After what seemed to be several minutes, the Primary president mercifully leaned over to my ear and whispered my lines, which I was able to repeat and then flee.

Speaking has never come naturally for me. It's something I've had to practice and learn, step-by-step, over many years. So, if you ever feel a sense of dread or anxiety at the thought of getting up to give a talk in church; if you're worried that people might fall asleep during your talk, or that you'll do something stupid; if you tend to procrastinate and then quickly cram together a talk at the last minute; if your mouth gets dry, your hands sweat, and you fear you'll to put your foot in your mouth; if you are so nervous that you're sure you can't possibly feel the Spirit as you talk—if you have any of these feelings, know this: you have a sympathetic friend in me. I've been through all those emotions. I've probably made every speaking mistake there is to make.

Once, early in my career, I was in the middle of a presentation and heard a thud. I looked up from my notes to see that someone had fallen asleep so soundly that they fell forward and hit their head on the chair in front of them! I've since learned how to not only keep people awake, but engaged and interested—you can too!

Since that traumatic Primary talk at the age of five, I've given over a thousand talks, presentations, and speeches, both in business and church settings. I've had the blessing of working with and observing many professional speakers and presenters, as well as learning from extraordinary church leaders.

Over the years, I've learned an amazing thing: being a great speaker is not something you're born with. People say,

"Good old Dennis—he's a born public speaker." Wrong. There are no born speakers. It's like saying someone is a born doctor. Personally, I'd rather have a trained doctor working on me—one who has acquired the skills and knowledge to diagnose and treat.[1] Speaking is the same. If you learn and practice the skills in this book, you'll discover that speaking is not as hard as you think it is. Soon, you will be able to speak calmly, powerfully, and effectively.

You've Been Asked to Speak in Church. Now What?

If you've received an assignment to speak in church, your first thought is probably to panic. Relax. You hold in your hands a simple, practical guide that will walk you, step-by-step, through the process. Speaking in church can actually be fun and enjoyable.

I promise that if you will read and follow the simple guidelines you'll find in this book, your talk will be amazing. Information + Skills + Practice = Success in anything you wish to accomplish. In this book, you will find the knowledge and skills you need to be a great speaker in church. The more you apply and practice these principles (as an active member of the Church, you'll have many opportunities to do so) you will become more polished and confident, and you will feel the guidance and help of the Lord.

1 Thanks to Mark Benson for this analogy.

The Top Ten Mistakes People Make Speaking in Church

As I've pondered the idea of writing this book, I've asked dozens of members this question: "What are the biggest mistakes people make when speaking in church?"

Here are the top ten answers:

1. **Reading** your whole talk.
2. **Going over** your allotted time. No one remembers what is said after the meeting should have ended.
3. **Planning too much** to be included in your talk. You can't cover seventeen points in a ten-minute talk.
4. **Talking too fast** without pauses or breaks.
5. **Being boring.** Not engaging your listeners through stories, examples, and enthusiasm.
6. **Random talking:** These talks have no organization or planning. The speaker is just talking aimlessly. Often the person wastes half their time telling how they were called to give the talk or telling a lame joke.
7. **Not connecting personally.** The topic is too broad and too sterile. It seems more like you are reading a research paper than giving a talk. Using too many scriptures or quotes, not enough personal stories and examples.
8. **Talking down** to the congregation or telling them how perfect you and your family are compared to others.
9. **Making inappropriate comments:** Bringing up topics that might be divisive or controversial, such as politics or a school football rivalry. This could also include vulgar language or slang words such as "crap," "sucks," or "bummed out" that may distract from the Spirit.

10. **Using worn-out material:** Nothing puts people to sleep faster than hearing stories or examples that are well used and everyone already knows. Even if the material is exceptional, if they have heard it over and over before, you will lose the audience. This includes reading large sections of someone else's talk instead of giving your own. Scripture stories are great, but even they can get old if told in the same way and the same few stories are used over and over.

Now, I don't wish to imply that all, or even most, of the talks we hear in church are awful. On the contrary, by and large, we have great speakers in the Church and our meetings are spiritually uplifting. I've also observed, as a participant in hundreds of business meetings for over twenty-five years, that our members are generally better speakers than many in the business community. This is most likely because we have opportunities to speak from a very young age. The purpose of this book is to help us to become even better.

It's clear from this list that we have some room for improvement. Sacrament meeting is the most important meeting in the Church, yet I can't ever remember having a class or instruction of any kind on how to give a great talk. Often, we just learn to speak by observing. Good or bad, the example we see in others often becomes the standard.

What Will You Learn in This Book?

We'll explore together how you can avoid the above mistakes so that you can plan, prepare for, and deliver a great talk in church—one where you feel comfortable, where you connect with the audience, and where the Spirit of the Lord can be present to teach and testify—a talk that people will remember and apply to their lives. Although we will focus mostly on speaking in sacrament meeting, many of the same principles can be applied to speaking in a conference or fireside, or even presenting a lesson in your quorum or class.

Since each principle builds on the previous one, you'll get the most out of this book by reading it cover to cover. However, if you're in a hurry or facing a speaking deadline, please feel free to skip around and pick out chapters and topics that you feel will help you right away. You'll find that key bits of information have been intentionally repeated throughout the book, so if you were to pick it up to review a specific element, you'll find everything you need right there.

You'll learn:

- How to avoid the top ten mistakes people make when speaking in church
- How to quickly plan and prepare an engaging talk, without hours of agonizing study
- How to connect with your listeners intellectually, spiritually, and emotionally
- How to speak with the companionship of the Spirit
- How to organize your talk so it's interesting and engaging

- How to remember your talk without reading or memorizing it
- How to discover and use personal stories of your own to illustrate gospel principles
- How to get their attention right away
- How to use stories to make your talks enjoyable and memorable
- How to move and inspire people to action
- How to overcome fear and anxiety about speaking in church
- How to speak with confidence and power
- And much more

I've learned how to overcome my hang-ups and develop the skills necessary to plan and deliver a great talk—not just one that gets compliments, but one that is entertaining and fun, leaves a powerful message, brings the Spirit, and changes lives. You will too.

Chapter 1

WHY SHOULD *YOU* TALK IN CHURCH?

As members of the Church, we are regularly given opportunities to speak, teach, and testify in our meetings. Perhaps you purchased this book because you have recently been asked to speak in church. You might be thinking: "Why me?" or "How did this happen?!"

What is the purpose for talking in church, anyway? Is it just to teach the principles of the gospel? Or is there something more? If the only reason for speaking in church is to transfer gospel knowledge, wouldn't it be more effective to just put on an audio CD of someone reading the scriptures, or set up a TV and replay some conference talks?

An even better question is: why should *you* talk in church? There must be something you have that no one else can offer in quite the same way—and there is. Everyone has unique talents, perspectives, and experiences that can benefit others. Each person is an individual spirit son or daughter of our Heavenly Father. You have a one-of-a-kind story that no one else can tell. You have a distinctive testimony that is unique to you.

Does Your Testimony Really Matter?

One Sunday, I heard the testimony of a young single adult named Emanuel. He was born into a Catholic family from Peru and enjoyed some spiritual experiences as a young man. However, he grew into a rebellious teen and was eventually sent to a military academy to shape up. Later, he decided to improve his relationship with God and considered becoming a Catholic priest. He learned about The Church of Jesus Christ of Latter-day Saints from a business associate, and after many experiences, met the missionaries and joined the Church.

His story of the winding road that eventually led him to the gospel was interesting and fresh. He was humble and unassuming, yet his testimony had a powerful effect on me. After the meeting, I went up to him and asked if he would be willing to write out his story and post it on a blog so others could read it. He agreed. Over the next few weeks, I helped him to write out the story of his conversion in clear language and post it where it could be read by thousands.

Here is an example of one comment a reader wrote after reading Emanuel's testimony online:

> "What strikes me most about your testimony, and what I believe is most compelling about this story, is the courage you show in telling it. It reeks of genuineness, honesty, and straight-forwardness, which is disarming and hard to attack or even taint. It lacks any guile, spin, or hidden agenda, leaving the reader

> unable to deflect, but completely exposed to the truth, and more importantly, the Holy Ghost. This story leaves little room for anyone to walk away from it with doubt as to the existence of Jesus Christ, and how He takes personal interest in our daily lives if we let him."[2]

Can anyone read this comment and then say, "My testimony doesn't matter?" The truth is: everyone's testimony matters. You may be the only one with the unique personality or background that allows you to touch a particular individual no one else can reach.

Several years ago when I was working with the full-time missionaries in our stake, a Japanese elder was assigned to our area. Elder Tateishi's family had moved from Japan to Brazil, where he grew up, and was later called on a mission to Salt Lake. He spoke fluent Japanese, some Portuguese, and very little English, but this elder had a desire to work and a burning testimony.

In our stake at the time, we were teaching a short, bubbly eighty-five-year-old woman by the name of Virginia Dillingham. Virginia had been born into an LDS family, but left the Church when she was in her thirties. Over the years, she had come into contact with many missionaries and had recently been taught by several sets of elders, but was still not ready to commit.

When Elder Tateishi came to our stake, his English was still not very good, so he misunderstood when he was told to teach Virginia the fourth discussion. Instead, he taught her the first discussion, which was just what she needed to hear

2 http://www.mormonblog.com/articles/24/1/147/The-Seed-of-Two-Members.htm

again. Even though the others attending the discussion could hardly understand Elder Tateishi's broken English, Virginia understood every word and was moved by the Spirit to the point that she made the decision to be baptized.

At Virginia's baptism, her daughter, Wendy, said, "Isn't it amazing how one little Japanese elder can change the whole outlook of a woman?"

Here was a woman who had studied the gospel for years and had been taught by numerous missionaries, but when this quiet, humble Japanese elder began teaching her, something struck a chord. This time it was different.

I don't know if there are any two people who had less in common than these two. She was a dynamic, outgoing, elderly, white American woman. He was a young, quiet, humble, Japanese man who grew up in Brazil. But there was a spiritual connection between them, and for some reason, he was the one who was able to spiritually connect with Sister Dillingham so the Holy Ghost could testify to her heart that she needed the gospel in her life.

What Can You Contribute?

From these and dozens of similar experiences, I have learned that everyone's testimony, perspective, and insights are important. As powerful as the prophet's testimony is, your individual story can be just as important in someone's life when your spirit touches theirs. For this reason, throughout the book, I will be encouraging you, and helping you, to discover your own voice—your own connection with the principles of the gospel—and to discover and share your own personal stories, experiences, and testimony.

People want to hear *your* talk, not someone else's. Rather than hearing what Bruce R. McConkie thinks about a gospel principle, the members of your ward would much rather hear what *you* think about it and how it has affected your life. That is why you are there. There's nothing wrong, of course, with using quotes from General Authorities to illustrate and support what you have said. Just be sure to start with your own unique insights and experiences—and share what they have taught you. Then, you can use quotes to reinforce your message.

We all wonder whether we personally have anything to contribute. A twelve-year-old deacon might doubt whether anything he could say would make a difference, and a ninety-two-year-old widow may feel that her time of usefulness and influence has past. Not so!

Here are some examples of how you can contribute and bless lives, no matter your stage in life:

Youth:

- You have a fresh, idealistic perspective
- You are the future of the Church
- You face temptations and challenges that are, in many ways, far beyond what adults face
- You have a different point of reference which makes your testimony unique
- You can state complex doctrines in easy-to-understand, modern language

- You have amazing spiritual strength
- You can motivate and inspire other youth to stay strong
- You have upbeat enthusiasm
- When youth give a great talk, everyone listens

Adults:

- You can teach and testify by your example—the way you live every day
- Your love and concern for your children and other youth opens hearts
- You are in the trenches, as it were, so your examples and teachings are practical and useful
- You can reflect on your past with the experience of maturity and see the hand of the Lord in shaping your life
- You carry heavy burdens, yet continue to rejoice in the blessings of the gospel
- Your understanding of the doctrines of the gospel has been deepened through study and expanded by the university of adversity
- You are aware of the dangers of the world and can sound a warning
- When adults give a great talk, everyone listens

Seniors:

- You have many years of experience and wisdom to draw upon
- You can tell interesting stories about your life and how you have learned the gospel

- You have faced challenges that may seem insurmountable today
- You can have a huge impact on the youth, who may be more likely to listen to a grandparent-type person than another adult who is their parent's age
- You have the time to contemplate the doctrines of the gospel and can offer amazing insights
- You are an anchor of stability in a changing world
- You are able to see patterns and dangerous trends others can't see
- When seniors give a great talk, everyone listens

Notice that the important thing is not our age or position in life. The important thing is that you give a "great talk." In this book, you will learn to do just that.

Personal Growth

In addition to what you can contribute, speaking is also very much a learning and growing experience for you. Stephen R. Covey taught, "You learn best when you teach another."[3] Your knowledge of the gospel grows as you try to teach it; your faith grows as you discover and share stories from your own life that illustrate God's love for you; and your testimony grows stronger each time you bear it. In short, you will learn and benefit just as much from the experience as those in the congregation will by hearing your talk.

3 The 8th Habit, Stephen R. Covey, Free Press: New York, 2005 p. 32

You Can Be a Spark in Someone's Life

One day several years ago, as we sat in a fast and testimony meeting, my wife, Marquette, felt a sudden prompting to tell how she first received her testimony of the Book of Mormon. She hadn't planned to do it, but she stood up and shared this experience. Later that morning, no fewer than five people came up to her and said, "Let me tell you about how I first got my testimony of the Book of Mormon." Her words had sparked a renewal of testimony in these individuals.

Recently, I climbed into our family van to go somewhere, put the key in the ignition, and turned it, but nothing happened. The van was completely dead. I soon found the reason. Someone had left a light on in the rear passenger area, which slowly drained the battery until there was nothing left. Fortunately, my wife was able to take me to my appointment in her car.

For the next several days, I would start walking to the van only to remember, "Oh, yeah, it's dead." Too busy to deal with it right then, I simply borrowed my wife's car. Finally the inconvenience was too much. I hooked up some jumper cables from her car to mine, and—voila! It started. I knew the battery was weak, so I left it running for the next couple of hours as the motor charged the battery. Pretty soon, my car was able to start without assistance.

Our testimonies are like a spiritual car battery. Sometimes there's a stress or drain on our spiritual battery, like leaving a light on, which slowly depletes the energy in our testimony until it is no longer able to function properly. When this happens, we are unable to dip into our own spiritual reservoir for strength; we may even fear that our testimony is dead. But a little spark from someone else—a heartfelt testimony or faith-promoting story—can immediately jump-start our testimony so it can begin to recharge and renew.

That is why you have been asked to talk in church. You can be that spark.

Chapter 2

CONNECTING WITH YOUR LISTENERS

Sacrament meeting is the most important and most sacred meeting of the week. If ever there was a meeting that deserved quality, engaging, Spirit-filled talks, this is it. Unfortunately all too often, sacrament meeting messages are filled with facts, but offer little opportunity for the audience to care about the topic or relate to the speaker. In this chapter, you'll learn how to forge a personal connection with your listeners so you can communicate intellectually, spiritually, and emotionally.

In the Doctrine and Covenants, the Lord asked a question of the Prophet Joseph Smith, saying, "Unto what were ye ordained?" In other words, why were you called? What are you supposed to do? The Lord answers His own question: "To preach my gospel by the Spirit, even the Comforter which was sent forth to teach the truth."[4]

In this simple statement, the Lord teaches some profound truths that beautifully apply to speaking in church. What are we called to do? First, we are to teach the truths of the gospel. And, second, we are to do so "by the Spirit."

4 D&C 50:13-14

A few verses later, the Lord clarifies what "by the Spirit" means and gives some powerful principles on speaking that will be a foundation for all that we discuss in this book. He explains:

> "He that receiveth the word by the Spirit of truth, receiveth it as it is preached by the Spirit of truth. Wherefore, he that preacheth and he that receiveth, *understand* one another, and both are *edified* and *rejoice* together."[5]

For years, people in the Church have used this scripture as a sort of cop-out, saying, "As long as I have the Spirit with me, it doesn't matter how boring my talk is" or "If the listeners have the Spirit, somehow the message will get through."

I choose to take a different approach. Of course it's important to have the companionship of the Lord's Spirit with us as we speak in church. But I believe the Lord is also telling us in this scripture that if we are truly speaking by the Spirit, we must make sure that three things occur: understanding, edification, and rejoicing. Anything we can do as the speaker to improve the experience of listening to a talk in church—by making our talks more interesting, engaging, and powerful—gives the Holy Ghost a much better opportunity to facilitate mutual understanding, edification, and rejoicing.

In my profession, I represent hundreds of business speakers and presenters. When an individual or a company asks for my advice in selecting training materials, I will invariably

5 D&C 50:21-22, emphasis added

recommend a presenter whose material is good but who also has exceptional presentation skills, rather than a speaker who has exceptional material but only average speaking skills. Why? People don't learn much when they're asleep!

Here is a cardinal rule that we will revisit over and over throughout the book:

As a speaker, it's not what you say,
but what gets through that's important.

This is true whether you're speaking in a business meeting, a political event, a community, function or in church. Boring talks that are poorly delivered, hard to hear, or given without enthusiasm offer little chance to get your message through, promote no connection with your audience, and provide limited opportunities for the Spirit to teach and testify.

The three elements in the above scripture—understand, edify, and rejoice—correspond to the three basic types of communication: intellectual, spiritual, and emotional. If you can learn how to connect on all three of these levels, you will truly be teaching by the Spirit and be able to move and inspire the congregation.

Like the three legs of a tripod which holds a camera steady, each of these elements must be in place in order to truly communicate with power. Take one away, and the communication falls down. For example, if your talk is intellectual and spiritual, but lacks any emotion or passion on the part of the speaker, it will not have a forceful or lasting impact. On the other hand, if you have plenty of emotion, but speak so quietly that it's difficult to hear—if the congregation is straining to hear and understand what you are saying—so much energy goes into grasping the meaning that the emotional and spiritual elements may not get through. Great sacrament meeting talks have all three levels of communication.

Let's look a little closer at these three elements that the Lord says are essential.

Understand—The Intellectual Connection

Understanding happens when members of the congregation are able to grasp the meaning of what you're saying—to understand the concepts. It's an intellectual transfer of knowledge. This is always the first goal of any teacher or speaker. In order to accomplish this, you need to organize and present your comments in a way that's easy to comprehend. (We'll learn more about organizing your talk in Chapter Four.) You must also speak with enough volume, confidence, and clarity that you can be heard and understood.

Edify—The Spiritual Connection

"Edify" is a fascinating word. It means to enlighten, uplift, nurture, and spiritually instruct. In the context of this scripture, I believe it means to strengthen and feed the spirit. We all need spiritual food on a regular basis—this is one of the major reasons we come to church each week. As speakers, we have the charge to spiritually feed the congregation, to build them up spiritually through our testimony and our faith. In other words, we are to "succor the weak, lift up the hands which hang down, and strengthen the feeble knees."[6]

How do you accomplish this in a church talk? It happens when our spirits connect with the spirits of the ward members. When we bear testimony and speak of our faith in Christ and His promises, there is a spiritual strength that flows back and forth between our spirits. We'll discuss this in more detail in a later section.

Rejoice—The Emotional Connection

Rejoicing refers to a purely emotional response. It means to be happy and cheerful, to delight in and to celebrate. This tells me that our talks should be enjoyable and enthusiastic—that when we speak, we should delight in the doctrines of the gospel. It means that our talks need to be a pleasant experience. It tells me that there is no excuse for talks that are dull, negative, mundane, or depressing. One of my favorite hymns begins: "Rejoice, the Lord is King." Yes, sacrament meeting should be a time of rejoicing over the triumph of Christ over death and sin, His unmatched gift of the Atonement, and the blessings and power that the gospel brings to each of our lives—this is certainly cause for joy and celebration.

6 D&C 81:5

I'm not suggesting that we should ever be irreverent or boisterous. That would be inappropriate and detract from the spirit of rejoicing. However, I am saying that our talks can be much more enthusiastic, upbeat, and enjoyable.

I've noticed that this feeling and attitude of rejoicing permeates our general conference meetings. Participants, especially the First Presidency and the Twelve, are upbeat, joyful, and energetic. This motivates us to want to improve and rededicate ourselves.

If your audience is to connect with you emotionally, you will have to learn to share your heart, not just information. This is important because there's a difference between hearing and caring.

Often, if we just give information, the subconscious response is, "So what?" In other words, unless they can sense that you really care about your topic, your audience may get the information, but not really care about it. But if you are passionate about your topic, if they can tell that you really care about it—and them—your listeners are much more likely to understand and internalize the information. In Chapter Three, we'll discuss ways to get passionate about your topic.

How do you connect emotionally in a church talk? The best way is to look people in the eye and to tell stories that have an emotional connection to you. The more you can share your heart in your talk, the more emotionally connected you will be with your listeners.

Spirit-to-Spirit Connection

Let's look at the above scripture again, this time focusing on different words.

> "He that preacheth *and* he that receiveth, understand *one another*, and *both* are edified and rejoice *together*."[7]

Notice that the experience must happen to both the speaker and the listener. Clearly, the Lord is teaching that there must be a personal connection between the speaker and the listener—spirit-to-spirit—in order to get our message across.

This spirit-to-spirit communication is an amazing process whereby one spirit can be touched, understood, and edified by another spirit through the power of the Holy Ghost. The Holy Ghost is not just a revelator, sending messages to you from God and testifying of truth—He is also a transmitter whereby He facilitates communication from one spirit to another. The prophet Nephi put it this way: ". . . when a man speaketh by the power of the Holy Ghost the power of the Holy Ghost carrieth it unto the hearts of the children of men."[8]

7 D&C 50:22, emphasis added
8 2 Nephi 33:1

In order to work properly, this kind of communication requires three separate spirits: the spirit of the speaker, the spirit of the receiver, and the Holy Ghost, which makes the communication possible. This, I believe, is one reason why you have been asked to get up and speak in church. No one else but you has your spirit, that eternal part of yourself that is a spirit daughter or son of God Himself, that unique entity with thoughts, talents, opinions, gifts, experiences, and insights that no one else has.

You can facilitate this spirit-to-spirit connection by speaking to each individual as if you are talking to them one-on-one. Make it a point to look people in the eye and hold their gaze for a few seconds as you speak so they know you are talking to them personally.

In addition, if members of the congregation are in tune with the Holy Ghost, they can receive inspiration that augments your spoken message. Have you ever thought, "This message is just for me" as you were listening to a talk? Have you had thoughts come to your mind which gave you additional insight or direction as someone was speaking? Perhaps this is the Holy Ghost telling you that this message is important for you, and then providing council and direction on how to apply the principles in your life.

The Power of the Word

As we improve our ability to teach the gospel through the Spirit, our words begin to have more impact upon the hearts of our listeners. Our words can, in fact, be more influential in motivating people to action than anything else, including world news, peer pressure, the economy, or even threats of physical force. Why? Because the Spirit carries it into the hearts of men and women.

I'm reminded of the story of Alma and the Zoramites in the Book of Mormon. In those days, when a group of people dissented from the Nephites, they often joined with the Lamanites and stirred up their hatred for the Nephites, resulting in wars and bloodshed. So, for the Nephites, helping people to return to the true faith was not just a matter of individual salvation, it was a matter of survival as a people.

For this reason, when the Nephites heard that the Zoramites, who lived on the borders of Lamanite territory, had separated themselves from the Nephites and were perverting the ways of the Lord, many Nephites were concerned that the Zoramites might become friendly with the Lamanites and lead an army back to try to destroy the Nephites. Some, I'm sure, wanted to send an army to prevent the Zoramites from separating (kind of like the American Civil War) and cut them off from the Lamanites.

Alma proposed a different approach. Listen to what he said:

> "And now, as the preaching of the word had a great tendency to lead the people to do that which was just—yea, it had had more powerful effect upon the minds of the people than the sword, or anything else, which had happened unto them—therefore Alma thought it was expedient that they should try the virtue of the word of God."[9]

Can a simple talk that you give in church have such a profound effect on the hearts of the men and women in your ward that it motivates them to change their lives, as Alma is suggesting? I think it can. In fact, the closer we are to the Spirit, and the more skillfully we can learn to prepare and present our talk, the more powerful our words become.

In this chapter, we've learned that we can move beyond just getting up and reading something in church—we can truly teach by the Spirit. As we improve our skills through proper preparation, organization, and presentation, we can learn to communicate intellectually, spiritually, and emotionally. Thus, speaking in church can be an experience of rejoicing together with the Saints.

Always our example in all things, Jesus Christ is the master speaker and teacher. As such, His words are filled with amazing power. Listen to this description:

---

9 Alma 31:5

"Behold, I am God: give heed unto my word, which is quick and powerful, sharper than a two-edged sword, to the dividing asunder of both joints and marrow; therefore give heed unto my words."[10]

This is our ultimate goal, to speak with such power.

10 D&C 6:2

Chapter 3

Content–Preparing Your Talk

Have you ever been asked to write a research paper for school? It's a pretty involved process. First, you do mountains of research on your assigned topic and narrow it down until you come up with a specific thesis—something you want to prove. Then, you organize your research to back up your thesis, stuffing it with as many facts as you can. In a research paper, the more quotes and citations you can use to back up your research, the better. Finally, you conclude by reviewing the research and stating how it backs up your thesis. Throughout the process, you are encouraged to remove any personal language or opinions from the paper so that it is objective and scholarly. For example, you must remove statements such as "I feel . . ." and replace them with objective statements like "The research shows . . ."

All too often, when someone is assigned to give a talk in church, say on faith, for example, they start by writing a research paper on faith. They read books and talks by General Authorities. They assemble a mountain of great notes, quotes, and scriptures. They organize their paper objectively and remove any personal opinions or thoughts.

Then they stand up in church and read their research paper.

This is the best recipe I can suggest for delivering a boring talk. It helps those who are sleep-deprived to get a needed snooze, but does little else. Why? Because the ingredients for a great research paper are totally different from what it takes to give a great talk.

Another approach to giving a talk is what I call randomness. This happens when speakers don't even organize their comments around a theme at all, but instead give a rambling hodgepodge of statements, thoughts, and comments that have nothing to do with each other or with the assigned topic. They may have great intentions, but what did they talk about? No one really knows.

If you've used any of these approaches before, you're not alone. I've done it too. In this chapter, you'll learn a better way to find and prepare your content. You'll learn ten steps to help you sift through your research, thoughts, and inspiration in a systematic way so you can prepare a great talk in a fraction of the time you may have spent before. Then, in Chapter Four, you'll learn how to organize it into a fabulous talk.

How do you decide what to say in your talk?

When you're given an assignment to speak, the biggest question that springs to your mind is often: what will you say? How do you get started? After reading the last chapter, you'll also be thinking: how will you find material that will help you to connect intellectually, spiritually, and emotionally?

Here are my ten steps for preparing the content of your talk:

1. Narrow the topic
2. Find your personal connection
3. Ponder and seek inspiration
4. Answer questions
5. Help your listeners to connect
6. Think of personal stories to illustrate your points
7. Start writing
8. Study and research
9. Determine your Anchor Statement
10. Develop your major points

Let's look at each of these steps in more depth.

#1 Narrow Your Topic

When you are asked to speak in sacrament meeting, you will normally be given a topic on which to speak. This helps to direct your thoughts and feelings as you begin to prepare. Often the topic is quite general and broad, which gives you the opportunity to narrow it down to a specific area within that topic that is interesting and personal. It also gives you the opportunity to follow the promptings of the Spirit as you decide what to say.

Here is an important key:

When selecting your topic, go deep instead of wide.

This means that instead of trying to cover as much of the topic as you can in your limited time, you should select one specific slice of the topic and teach it in depth.

Let's say, for example, that you were asked to speak on charity. Look at the illustration on the opposite page. Charity encompasses so many elements that there is no way that you can cover all aspects of charity in a fifteen-minute sacrament meeting talk.

Yet, we've all seen speakers try to do it. They might start by giving the dictionary definition of charity and listing some of its elements. In order to get it all in, they have to make their talk so general and shallow that they never get beyond the intellectual level to add the emotional or spiritual legs of communication.

Great speakers, on the other hand, consider all of the different aspects of charity and then choose one that is particularly meaningful to them. This allows them the time to go deep into that narrow topic and fill their talk with interesting examples, personal stories, and observations that make it live in the hearts, minds, and spirits of the ward members.

Remember, it's better to get across one solid point that changes lives than to list ten points with little impact.

If you're not sure right now which narrow slice of your topic you want to select, don't worry. Just move on to the next steps, which will help you to select and narrow your topic and to come up with supporting points, stories, and applications to make your talk great.

Never Give Up On People
Submit as a Child
Serve as Inspired by Holy Ghost
Generous with Money
Compassion
Evidence of Testimony
Love Your Neighbor
Unfailing Love
Selfless
PATIENT
Kind
Pray for Charity
Humble Service
Take food to Home Bound
Pure Love Of Christ
A Gift of God
Charity
Lifting Spirits
Caring for the poor
DISCIPLES LOVE ONE ANOTHER
Not Happy About Bad Things
Not Easily Provoked
Long Suffering
How to Develop Charity
Not Envious
Forgiving Those Who Have Wronged Us
Give Time
Christ-like Attribute
RESPECTFUL
Visiting the Sick
Charity at Home
Rejoice in Truth
Not Judging
CHARITY IN A NEIGHBORHOOD
Going After the One

#2 Find Your Personal Connection

Now look at your topic from an emotional and spiritual point of view. It's an opportunity for you to determine what part of the topic you feel most passionate about. Think about this:

If you don't particularly care about what you are saying, neither will your listeners.

The more connected you can be to your material, the more the ward members will feel that connection themselves.

Remember, the only thing people really listen to is your personal passion. Narrow your topic until you find something that you can be enthusiastic about. Open up to your feelings and discover what truly moves you. Share your authentic perspective as it relates to your topic. The more personally connected you are to your topic, the more earnest you will be and the more powerfully you will articulate your message.

Questions to ask yourself:

- What part of this topic is the most interesting to me?
- What part don't I understand that I would like to learn more about?
- In what way am I passionate about this subject?
- Of what part do I have the strongest testimony? How did I get that testimony?
- What specific part of this principle used to be difficult for me, but is now easier?

- How do I want members of the congregation to feel after they hear my talk? What do I want them to do?
- How can I teach this subject on an intellectual, emotional, and spiritual level?

#3 Ponder, Pray, and Seek Inspiration

Once, our ward Relief Society presidency was asked to speak in sacrament meeting. Each of the four speakers received the same general topic: renewal. They individually approached the Lord for guidance on how, specifically, to approach the subject.

Independently, they each decided that one part of renewal is having the spiritual strength to move forward in the face of adversity. Each speaker approached this narrow topic from her own perspective so the talks supported and augmented each other. It was clear to everyone that the Lord wanted this message delivered to the ward members at this time, and He harmonized the talks so this principle would be beautifully taught from a variety of perspectives. This is a pattern the Lord uses over and over to teach His Saints.

In general conference, no topics are given. Each speaker must approach the Lord for guidance on what to say. Yet, as spiritual guidance is received, coordinated themes naturally develop that can only be attributed to the inspiration of the Spirit. Speaking of this phenomenon, Elder Neil L. Anderson said:

> "There are no assigned subjects, no collaboration of themes. The Lord's way, of course, is always the best way.

> He takes the individual prayerful efforts of each speaker and orchestrates a spiritual symphony full of revelation and power. Repeated themes, principle building upon principle, prophetic warnings, uplifting promises—the divine harmony is a miracle!"[11]

What does this mean for you as you prepare to speak in sacrament meeting? I urge you to spend as much time on your knees praying and pondering as you do studying in the scriptures or other books. Sacrament meeting talks are very important to the Lord. If you will approach Him in faith, He will inspire you with insights, stories, and inspiration about what to say.

Speaking about Nephi and Lehi (the sons of Helaman) the scriptures affirm: ". . . they had power and authority given unto them that they might speak, and they also had what they should speak given unto them."[12]

The Lord gives a similar promise in Doctrine and Covenants Section 100, where He declares:

> Lift up your voices unto this people; speak the thoughts that I shall put into your hearts, and you shall not be confounded before men; For it shall be given you in the very hour, yea, in the very moment, what ye shall say.[13]

11 Tell Me the Stories of Jesus, Neil L. Andersen, April 2010 Conference
12 Helaman 5:18, emphasis added
13 D&C 100:5-6

This scripture should not be taken as an excuse to avoid planning and preparing our talks. The Lord is not saying, "Don't study and prepare." He is not saying, "Don't think about better ways to present the gospel; don't seek My help; don't plan, prepare, or polish your messages." He is not saying, "Just stand up with a blank mind and I'll do all the work for you."

Listen to what the Lord said to Hyrum Smith:

> Seek not to declare my word, but first seek to obtain my word, and then shall your tongue be loosed; then, if you desire, you shall have my Spirit and my word, yea, the power of God unto the convincing of men.[14]

Clearly, we need to study, plan, and prepare our messages. Then, through the Spirit, it will be given to us, in the very moment if necessary, which of our prepared messages we should give to touch a particular individual. Further, only when we have sufficiently studied and prepared can we reasonably expect to have His Spirit and to speak with power.

#4 Answer Questions

What questions might people have about your topic? One of the best exercises you can do as you plan your talk is to sit down with a piece of paper and, for fifteen minutes, just write out as many questions as you can think of about this topic.

14 D&C 11:21

Don't try to answer the questions at this point—just write as many questions as you can. You'll find that this exercise provides a ton of interesting potential material for your talk.

You should also consider what questions the ward members might ask themselves as you speak and then integrate the answers into your message to make it more engaging.

For example, I once visited a ward where the speaker mentioned that he was a recent convert to the Church, having been baptized just five years earlier, and noted that this was the first time he had spoken in church since his baptism. He then went on to talk about some principles of the gospel he believed in and to bear his testimony. I'm sure I was not the only person in the congregation thinking, "I wonder how he learned about the Church." His testimony was great, but I would love to have heard the story of his conversion.

The same is true for missionaries who speak in sacrament meeting upon their return. We're thrilled to have them teach and testify. It's wonderful to see that they have grown in faith and gospel knowledge, but what we really want to know is how their faith and testimony grew. What happened in the mission field that has effected this mighty change in them? How did the message of the gospel affect the lives of the people they met? Returned missionaries are often given an assigned gospel topic. This is as it should be. But there's no reason why they can't use stories and examples from their missionary service to teach gospel principles and strengthen our faith.

Another way to prepare is to pretend that there will be a question and answer period following your talk. Try to anticipate what questions might be asked. Is it possible that someone might disagree with what you're saying? If so, try to pinpoint what their objections would be and then answer them as you give your talk.

Here are some general questions that members of the congregation might ask:

- How did you first gain a testimony of this principle?
- Why have you been asked to talk about this topic? What insights can you share with me?
- What challenges have you overcome that can give me hope in my life?
- Was it always easy for you to follow this principle?
- Why do you really come to church each week?
- How do you stay strong with all the challenges you face?
- Why should I listen to you?
- How does this apply to me?
- So what?

#5 Help Listeners to Connect: Intellectually, Emotionally, and Spiritually

The last question in the above list is probably the number one question on people's minds when they hear someone speak. "So what?" they ask. "Do you really have something to say? Will it be interesting? Does it apply to me?"

This is particularly true if the people in the audience don't know you personally. If you are a member of the ward where you are speaking, they will often give you the benefit of the doubt and listen because they love you. However, if you are speaking to a group that you don't know well, such as at stake conference or a fireside, they will ask, "So what?" That's why giving talks is so much more difficult for high councilors, and could be one reason why they have a reputation for giving "dry" talks.

Instead of "So what" you want to get people thinking, "Me too!" This drops the barrier so you can really communicate. I learned this concept from a captivating business speaker named Jim Rohn. You can get your listeners thinking, "Me too!" by sharing a story or experience they can relate to, one that involves them emotionally and puts them into the story.

Try to tell the story from the listener's point of view. Use "you" instead of "I" as often as you can when telling the story. That places them in the action.

Here's an example from my own life that I used in a recent talk. Watch how the listener is immediately placed in the story and then drawn in emotionally. I call it "The Story of the Apricot Tree."

> If you came to my house when I was a little boy, you would have seen a huge apricot tree in our back yard which towered over all the other trees in the neighborhood. In the spring, it was covered with white blossoms. As Primary children, when we would sing, "I looked out the window

and what did I see? Popcorn popping on the apricot tree," I figured someone in the Primary had been to our house and had written a song about our tree. It was so large that we built a three-story tree house in it—partly to play in, and partly to help pick the thousands of apricots each fall. I know there were thousands, because I had to pick them. We made apricot jam, apricot leather, apricot chicken, apricot nectar, and apricot ice cream.

The best part about our tree, however, was the large sandbox my father had built under the entire tree, with the trunk sticking up in the center.

Our favorite thing to do was play in the sandbox with water. We would string several hoses together in order to bring water from the house all the way back to the tree. There, we would put the hose near one corner of the sandbox and let it run. Pretty soon, we would have a little river. We used the wet sand to build cities, farms and castles (complete with a moat). As the water rose, our cities needed higher walls to protect them from flooding. Soon, where there used to be rivers and lakes, there were now great oceans. Eventually, the whole sandbox was flooded, and we would be done until another day.

We would return home wet and covered in sand from head to foot. (I still have a little sand in my hair from those wonderful summer days.) Often, when we tried to enter the house, Mother would say, "Stop!" Then, she would march us out in back where she would line us up and hose us down to get all the wet sand off.

My brothers and sisters and I lived in that house for eighteen years. The summer after we moved, the apricot tree died.

I've often thought about that apricot tree. Never have I seen a tree that large bear so much fruit. It thrived, despite hundreds of big nails being driven into it. (I'm

> very thorough when I build a tree house.) As I have analyzed it over the years, I think it must have been all that water saturating the roots of the tree as we were playing with water in the sandbox that made the difference. Of course, we didn't realize what we were doing at the time, but it had an effect, nevertheless. Then, when the water was no longer there, the tree died.
>
> A similar thing happens when we saturate our homes and families with the gospel of Jesus Christ. As we do, we will, like my apricot tree, be able to thrive, no matter the difficulties or challenges we face.

What are some of the elements in this story that draw in the members of the congregation so they are participating emotionally in the story?

First, it describes playing as a child, bringing up happy feelings of carefree summers, playing outside, getting dirty, and building a fort or tree house. Second, it describes losing something that is important to us. In my case, it was my apricot tree, which represented the joy of youth. We've all lost things. It may have been something trivial, like car keys or a watch; others mourn major losses, such as the death of a loved one or the loss of virtue. This brings up tender emotions which connect your listeners with the story—and with you.

No one can tell that story with the same emotion as I can tell it. Why? Because I experienced it myself, it's my story, and that comes across in the delivery. This is why in Chapter Six, when we discuss stories in detail, I'll encourage you to discover and tell your own stories. Even if you read someone else's story word for word, you will never capture the emotion as well as they did—because it's not yours.

In addition to connecting emotionally, this story illustrates the intellectual message of the talk, which was, "We can have the strength to weather any challenge by saturating our lives with the gospel."

At the end, when I tie the story to Christ and His gospel, the Spirit testifies to our hearts that the principle is true. Thus, the listeners and I have communicated intellectually, spiritually, and emotionally.

Here's another example of how stories establish an emotional connection in order to change "So what?" to "Me too!"

David was king of Israel. Everywhere he went, people bowed down to him and did whatever he wanted. But David had sinned, and the Lord sent the prophet Nathan to rebuke him.

If Nathan had come to David and started preaching to him, telling him how much he had disappointed the Lord, what do you think David's response would have been?

I'm confident he would have thought, "I'm the great king of Israel. The princes of the earth bow down before me. Who are you to tell me what to do?" I'm confident David would have thought, "So what?"

But Nathan didn't do that. He knew he needed to get David thinking with him before he could call him to repentance. Nathan also had good reason to fear for his own life.

So, Nathan came to David and simply launched into a story. Here it is:

> There were two men in one city; the one rich, and the other poor. The rich man had exceeding many flocks and herds: But the poor man had nothing, save one little ewe lamb, which he had bought and nourished up: and it grew up together with him, and with his children; it did eat of his own meat, and drank of his own cup, and lay in his bosom, and was unto him as a daughter.
>
> And there came a traveler unto the rich man, and [instead of taking] of his own flock and of his own herd, to dress for the wayfaring man that was come unto him; [the rich man] took the poor man's lamb, and dressed it for the man that was come to him.
>
> And David's anger was greatly kindled against the man; and he said to Nathan, As the Lord liveth, the man that hath done this thing shall surely die: And he shall restore the lamb four fold, because he did this thing, and because he had no pity.[15]

Notice that not only did the story have David's attention, it aroused his emotion as well. David was in the story; he was thinking, "Me too." Now it was time to teach.

"And Nathan said to David, Thou art the man." In essence, he told him: "You have done what the man in the story did. The Lord gave you everything, from your kingdom to your wives and family. But you were not content. You killed a man and took his wife for your own."

How did David react to this rebuke? He admitted his sin and began to repent.

---

15 Samuel 12:1-13

Remember, as long as people are thinking "So what?" very little of what you say will get through. Only when they begin thinking, "Me too," can you truly begin to teach with any impact.

This emphasizes our rule from the last chapter:

It's not what you say, but what gets through that's important.

#6 Think of Personal Stories

Notice that in both the examples above, the thing that changed "So what?" into "Me too!" was a story. Stories are one of the most powerful teaching tools we have and they are the center point of any good talk. Stories transport us to a different time and place. They paint pictures in our minds that become an anchor for gospel doctrines.

Think about your own experiences. What conference talks are the most memorable to you? Chances are they had great stories to illustrate the point. Who can forget Elder Bednar's parable of the pickle or President Uchtdorf's stories about flying an airplane? These apostles don't just tell stories so we'll be entertained. They do it so we'll be engaged and remember the message. When we remember the stories, we also remember the gospel application.

Each Sunday afternoon when our children were young, as we sat around the dinner table, we would ask them, "What did you learn in church today?" or "What was your favorite talk in sacrament meeting?" Invariably, they would remember a story someone used in a talk or lesson. After they repeated the story, we would ask, "What did you learn from it?" Then, they would remember the principle they learned. It was the story that made the point memorable.

In Chapter Six, we'll spend an entire chapter together learning how you can come up with stories from your own life and use them to make your talk compelling.

#7 Start Writing

At this point, you should start writing down all your personal thoughts and ideas about the topic. What is your unique connection with the subject? Record any inspiration you felt or changes in direction you experienced along the way. Look at the questions you wrote in step four and try to answer those that are pertinent to your topic. List the important points you want to make. Write down your feelings and note the stories or examples that have come to mind as you pondered your talk.

The important thing here is to simply start writing. Don't worry about organizing everything or making it perfect at this point. Getting your thoughts on paper will give you confidence that you personally have something to say.

#8 Study and Research

Many speakers make the mistake of doing this step first when they write a talk. Unfortunately, by jumping too quickly into outside sources, they often lose their personal thoughts, insights, stories, and ideas. This is why I encourage you to pursue steps one through seven first. It helps you preserve your unique perspective and prevents your talk from becoming simply a string of General Authority quotes. Once you have recorded your personal insights in step seven, begin studying other sources to add depth and background to your talk.

In this step, you'll study the scriptures, church magazines, books, and other resources to find information about your topic. Dale Carnegie said that "Speakers should know forty times more about their topic than they share in their presentation."[16] The more you can learn, the more confident you will be.

An important, yet often overlooked, resource is other people. You can gain valuable insights by asking people what your topic means to them and hearing their stories and examples.

As you study outside sources, you'll add more notes, scriptures, quotes, and ideas to what you've already written. You'll also have additional examples and stories come to mind. This gives you more material to draw from, but it can lead to a dangerous trap—planning too much in your talk. Here is an important rule:

16 Stand And Deliver, Simon & Schuster Audio, Dale Carnegie Training, 2007

You don't have to use all of the information you collect in your talk.

In fact, most of the information you assemble will never be used. You might collect 20 scriptures and only use one, or find 10 quotes and not use any. The purpose for researching and studying is not to collect as many facts as you can about the topic and then "wow" the audience with your superior knowledge. Instead:

1. Studying can be a catalyst for revelation. Remember the story of Lehi in the Book of Mormon—he was commanded to send his sons to obtain the brass plates, the scriptures. When they finally brought the plates to him and he began to read them, "he was filled with the Spirit."[17] As you read and study, you too will be filled with the Spirit and have thoughts come to your mind that will guide you in the direction your Heavenly Father would like you to take. You will also discover your own spiritual and emotional connections with the principle you are studying.
2. Studying is a testimony builder. If you don't currently have a testimony of a particular principle, you can study various aspects of it until something sparks or resonates with you. You can then talk about this journey of discovery and describe how it has affected you.
3. Studying helps you verify that your talk is in harmony with church doctrine. Make sure that your comments

17 1 Nephi 5:10,17

correlate with what the scriptures and current church leaders say about your topic. Few things are as distracting (as well as confusing) to your listeners as hearing something that is a little off base doctrinally. It can also drive out the Spirit because the Holy Ghost can't testify to something that's not true.

4. Studying gives you confidence and passion for your subject. The deeper you delve into a topic that appeals to you, the more interesting it will become and the more prepared you will feel to talk about it.
5. Studying crystallizes your thinking. It helps you to solidify and flesh out your unique perspectives and insights.
6. Studying helps you identify the best scriptures or quotes to support your message.

#9 Determine Your Anchor Statement

In this step, you will attempt to describe in one sentence what you want your listeners to internalize and remember about your talk. This is the major take-home lesson. Like an anchor that keeps a ship from drifting off into dangerous waters, your Anchor Statement keeps you on track as you assemble materials for your talk. Remember, you only have limited time, usually ten to twenty minutes, to make your point. You can't afford to drift off into areas that don't contribute to your central message.

A well-crafted Anchor Statement is the focal point of your message and helps the members of the congregation to figure out what you are saying. Take the time to hone and polish your Anchor Statement so it clearly articulates the idea in as few words as possible. Craft it in such a way that it demonstrates your passion for the topic and motivates people to action. Your Anchor Statement should make your listeners think, "How?" or "Why?"

For example, let's assume you were assigned to speak on missionary work. In steps one and two above, you might decide that the slice of this topic that you are most passionate about is: being a friend and example to everyone. So, you might start with an Anchor Statement like this:

> "One way that we can be good missionaries is by being friends with everyone we come in contact with and setting a good example for those around us."

Now reduce and clarify your Anchor Statement so it's shorter and the meaning is crystal clear:

"Missionary work starts with being a sincere friend and a good example."

Notice that this Anchor Statement is short enough to be easily remembered. The scope is also narrow enough that you can spend the bulk of your talk giving specific points and stories that directly support this statement intellectually, spiritually, and emotionally.

The goal is to make your point so clear that if a latecomer walked up to a member of the congregation and asked, "What was the talk about?" they would respond without hesitation, "How missionary work starts with being a sincere friend and a good example."

In order to achieve this goal, make sure that your content and structure directly support your Anchor Statement. Be sure to include elements that communicate your message emotionally and spiritually, as well as intellectually, in your talk. As you do, ward members are more likely to be motivated to respond to the query with action phrases such as, "I need to be more obedient and prayerful so my faith in Christ will be stronger."

When this happens, you have not only given a great talk, you have changed someone's life.

If you're still not sure what your Anchor Statement should be, you could work backwards by deciding which stories you want to tell, then determining what they mean (what is the point of each story?) and finally distilling all your points together into your Anchor Statement.

#10 Develop Your Major Points

Now, look at all the material you have collected: thoughts, quotes, stories, examples, and scriptures. Sift through it and decide on the major points you want to make to support your Anchor Statement, which should make them ask how or why.

In the above example, the following questions might spring to mind:

> "Why are friendship and example important for missionary work?"
> "How can I do missionary work by being a friend and setting a good example?"

You might decide to use the points of your talk to answer these questions.

Each point should be illustrated by a story or example as its central feature. This adds the emotional and spiritual connections to your talk. Sort through all the stories, examples, and quotes you have collected and choose the ones that best teach the concept. Remember our rule from earlier in this chapter:

You don't have to use all of the information you collect in your talk.

You may have found a moving story that you like, but it doesn't quite fit in with your Anchor Statement. I recommend that you leave it out. Just save it in your file of stories for another occasion.

Along with the story, you'll want to write down a few ways that ward members can apply this point in their lives. You might also select one scripture or quote that forcefully drives the point home.

Using the example above, if your Anchor Statement is: "Missionary work starts with being a sincere friend and a good example," one of your points might be:

"Your example can spark gospel interest in others."

Perhaps you have an interesting story about someone who asked you a question because they observed you living a principle of the gospel. After telling the story, you would complete the point by giving a couple of ideas, and perhaps a scripture or quote, on how we can be good examples of the believers.

Now that you have completed the ten steps, you should have a pretty good idea of what you want to say in your talk. Here are a few additional points to keep in mind.

Consider Your Audience

It's easy to assume that everyone in the congregation is at the same level of gospel knowledge, or that we all have the same degree of spiritual strength. But this is not necessarily the case.

Congregations are diverse and may include brand-new members to those who grew up in the Church. Among your listeners could be people not of our faith who are investigating the Church, as well as members whose faith is undeveloped or whose challenges seem crushing. There will be widows seeking solace, teenagers facing worldly temptations, parents struggling to provide for their families, and individuals searching for hope.

I've personally had periods in my life when things were so difficult that I came to church praying to find something—some glimmer of hope—that would get me through the next week.

As a speaker, please keep the needs of these individuals in mind. A good rule of thumb is to speak as if someone who is not a member of our church is sitting in the congregation. Avoid LDS jargon that might not be familiar to them and stay away from topics that are speculative or represent fringe areas of the gospel. Our job is to preach the fundamental doctrines in an uplifting and personal way.

Always keep in mind that sacrament meeting should be a spiritual experience for all participants. As a speaker, everything you do should be in harmony with, and never detract from, the sacred nature of the sacrament. "Talks and music should focus on gospel subjects that help members build faith and testimony."[18]

What about Humor?

Can humor have a place in a sacrament meeting talk? Yes, of course, it can. However, it should never detract from the sacred nature of the meeting. Light-hearted moments add emotional release and connection with

18 Handbook 2, Administering the Church 18.2.2, 2010

your listeners. They make your talk fun and enjoyable. The Lord has commanded us to "be of good cheer,"[19] and this instruction applies even in sacrament meeting.

However, humor should not be attempted for its own sake, such as telling an unrelated joke at the beginning of your talk. If humor is natural for you, make it part of your talk in a way that contributes to the overall message. If humor is not part of your natural makeup, leave it out. Just present your talk with enthusiasm, and it will be great. If your attempt at humor is awkward or distasteful, it can detract from your message. Never make fun of other people in order to lighten up your talk. If someone must be the brunt of your humor, be sure it's you. People enjoy a light-hearted rendition of a minor blunder—just make sure it relates to your message.

There is a difference between being light-hearted and being light-minded. Light-heartedness could be defined as happy, cheerful, joyful, not taking self too seriously. Light-mindedness, on the other hand, is mocking or making light of sacred things and should never be a part of a sacrament meeting talk.

Keep it Positive

I once heard a talk given by a very scholarly man. He spoke of the many evils in the world. He used scripture after scripture to dwell on the wickedness of mankind and our fallen nature. He indicated that most of the inhabitants of

19 Matthew 14:27

the world will be thrust down to hell and quoted passages which indicated that even many of the elect—members of the Church—will fail to reach their goal of exaltation because of their sinful nature.

There was no mention of Christ and His triumph over the world or the power of the Atonement in our lives.

It was the most depressing talk I have ever heard. I think many went away thinking, *I'll never make it, I might as well give up.*

This talk may have been technically correct. After all, he used numerous scriptures and quotes by General Authorities to make his points. But the tone of the talk was completely out of line with the message of the gospel of Jesus Christ. The word gospel means "good news." It is a message of joy and hope.

Think about the talks we receive in general conference. Do they dwell on the problems, or do they focus on the solution? Do they make you feel hopeless, or do they encourage you to commit to be better? The answer, of course, is that conference messages always focus on the solution, which is Christ and His gospel.

Your primary purpose for speaking in church is to encourage the Saints to want to improve and to build their faith and testimony. One question we mentioned earlier bears repeating here:

How do you want members of the congregation to feel after they hear your talk?

If you want them to feel encouraged, hopeful, and determined to do better, you'd better make sure that your talk supports those kinds of feelings. Make it your goal that your listeners will walk away from your talk thinking, "I can!"

"I can improve my life through the gospel."

"I can hold on a little longer."

"I can put my trust in Christ."

The Apostle Paul put it this way, "I can do all things through Christ which strengtheneth me."[20]

No matter what your topic, that is the message you want to portray.

Organizing Your Talk

Well done! You've decided what you are going to say, which is the hardest part of preparing your talk. In the next chapter, you will learn how to plug your information into an easy-to-use structure that will make your talk flow naturally and powerfully.

---

20 Philippians 4:13, emphasis added

Chapter 4
Structure—Organizing Your Talk

Now that you have decided what you want to say and planned some of the important elements, such as your major points, stories, and applications, you are ready to organize them into a real talk.

In this chapter, you will learn a simple structure you can use to easily and quickly organize your talk so it will be both powerful and memorable.

Some might think that having an organized structure could make your talk inflexible, but just the opposite is true. When you organize your talk as described below, you will be able to adjust the time of your talk, rearrange the elements for maximum impact, and you'll also leave room for the Lord to inspire you to add or remove something. Rather than preventing revelation, preparation and organization actually encourage it.

Look at the chart on page 63. This gives you a quick visualization of your talk. It may look a little intimidating at first. Don't worry. We'll go through it a step at a time. I think you'll discover that when it comes to organizing and remembering your talk, this structure chart is your best friend.

All you need to do is plug in pieces of content you collected in the last chapter, practice a few times, and you're ready to go. You'll find a blank version of this chart in the appendix that you can copy and use for your talk. Simply write key words and phrases in each shape to remind yourself of what you will say in each section of your talk. If you are using a scripture or General Authority quote, you can write it in the margin or on the back of your chart to make sure you quote it correctly.

Once you have practiced your talk a few times, this chart could be all that you need to take to the pulpit. Even if you take your other notes with you (for security—just in case) you will probably not need to refer to them. As long as you know what you want to say in each section, you have essentially learned your talk.

Best-selling speaker and media personality Dian Thomas says that you should "make a mental picture of your talk" so you will always know where you are and what you want to say next. This chart makes it easy to do just that.

Plugging elements into the structure chart is like mixing a recipe. If you add all the right ingredients, in the right order, it makes something yummy—every time. This chart is the same. If you use it as described below, it will be an invaluable tool to help you organize, remember, and present your talk.

You might ask, "If members follow this speaking chart, won't all church talks be the same from now on?"

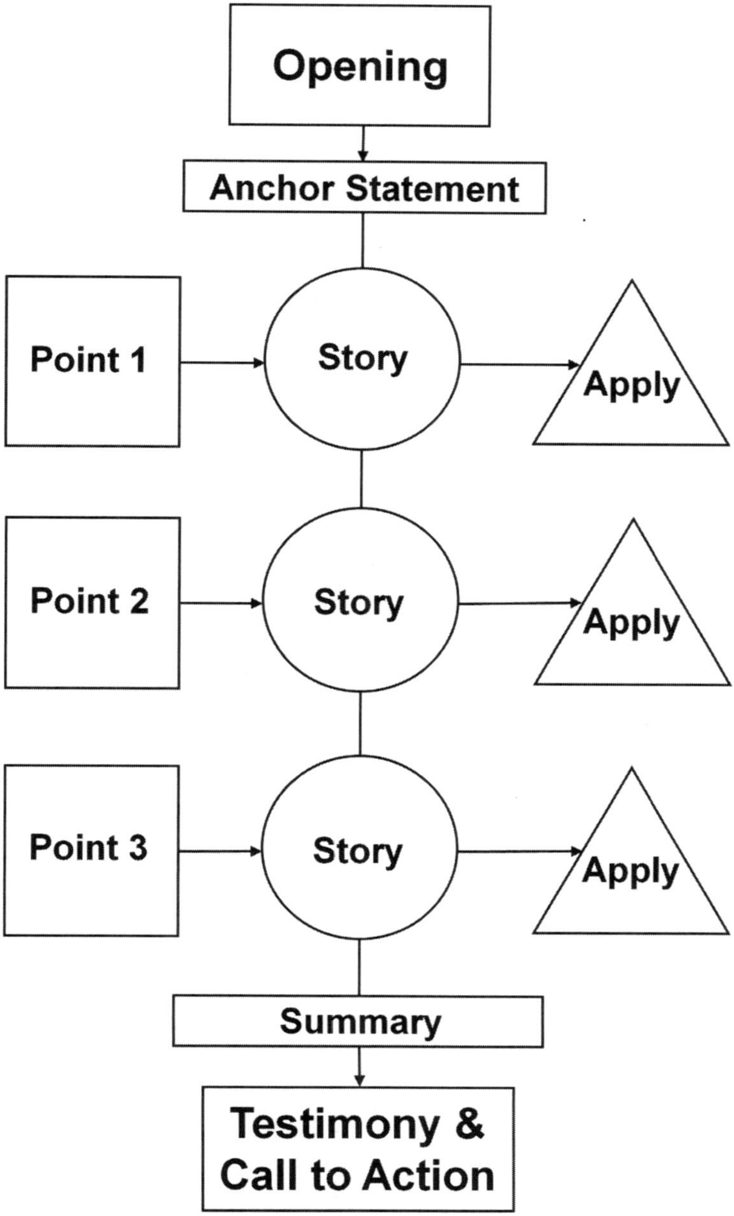
Opening
Anchor Statement
Point 1
Story
Apply
Point 2
Story
Apply
Point 3
Story
Apply
Summary
Testimony &
Call to Action

Of course not! Each person has his or her own speaking style and there is enough flexibility in each element to let your unique voice shine through. The structure gives your talk a more effective and organized flow without sacrificing individuality.

As you observe good speakers in the Church, you'll find that they generally follow a similar pattern so this concept is not new or revolutionary. The chart just provides you with an easy-to-use, visual structure with which to build your talk.

Let's look at the different elements one at a time:

Opening

Start strong with a great Opening. Other than your closing Testimony and Call to Action, this is the most important part of your talk. It sets the tone and dictates the congregation's expectations for the rest of your talk.

In the first two minutes, you tell your listeners whether your talk will be worth listening to, or if they should catch a few winks. This is also the point when you tend to be the most nervous. If you can give it well, it will boost your confidence so you can relax and give the rest of your talk.

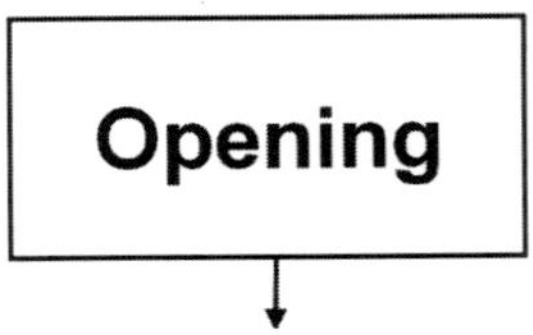

For this reason, you should know exactly what you will say in your Opening and rehearse it more than any other part of your talk so you can stand up and deliver it with confidence.

This element is so important that Chapter Five is entirely devoted to developing a strong Opening statement, including numerous examples of ways to start off on the right foot.

The two most important things to remember about the Opening are:

1) The way you open determines how much attention you will get for the rest of your talk—so start strong.
2) Your opening must relate to the subject of your talk.

Anchor Statement

As we learned in the previous chapter, all great talks have a concise Anchor Statement as their foundation—one sentence that represents the overall take-home message you want to settle in the hearts, minds, and spirits of your listeners. Make sure you articulate it in such a way that your listeners can feel why it's important for them personally.

The Anchor Statement is the overriding guide for everything you say so you don't start drifting off topic. Every point, story, example, or application in your talk should support it. Even though the message of your Anchor Statement may be clear from the context of your talk, it's still a good idea to state it. This increases their desire to pay attention to see if you can deliver on your statement.

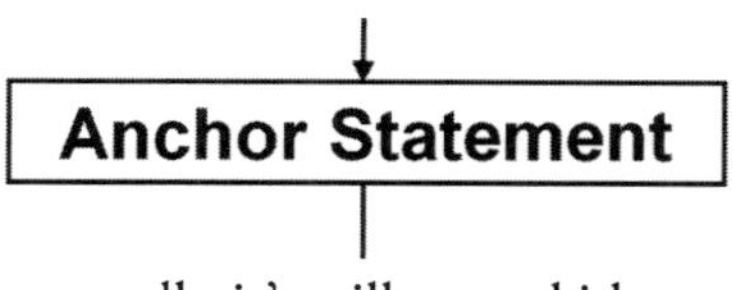

Your Anchor Statement not only indicates what you want the members of the congregation to learn, it includes what you want them to feel and do. The more clear, specific, and concise your statement is, the more powerful your talk will be.

Point Groups

Next in the structure chart, you will find three Point Groups identified as Point – Story – Apply. This is a concept I learned from Joel Weldon, one of the finest public speakers alive today, and a master storyteller. Simply stated, you organize each section of content so that you 1) state your point 2) tell a story or give an example that illustrates the point, and 3) help the audience apply it to their lives by reviewing the lessons learned in the story. Then you do the same thing with your second point, and your third.

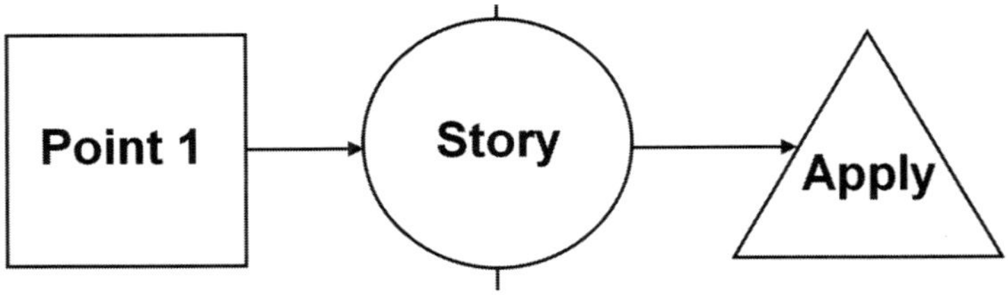

Why only three? In a sacrament meeting talk of ten to twenty minutes, that's all you'll have time for. If you are a youth speaker, you'll likely only have time for one point.

This is the beauty of organizing your talk with this structure chart. The points build upon and support each other, and collectively they work together to teach the Anchor Statement. But each point group is also a stand-alone section of your talk. If time runs short, as it often does, you can eliminate one or two of your point groups and still have an excellent, cohesive talk.

I've even given a talk where I eliminated all of the points and just gave the Opening (which was a short story), the Anchor Statement, Summary, and Testimony—and it worked out fine. It was enjoyable, I still got my major idea across, and I was able to finish in three minutes so we could end on time.

Point

As you are preparing your content, you may come up with seven, ten, or even twenty Points that you want to make in your talk. Now that you have reduced and clarified your Anchor Statement, the time has come to carefully select the three most important Points you want to make that will best support

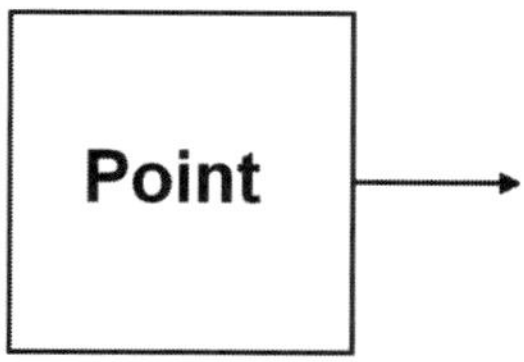

the Anchor Statement. As mentioned above, each Point should be accompanied by a Story and the Application of the point in our lives. Often the best way to select your points is to choose the ones for which you have the most interesting and moving personal stories.

As with the Anchor Statement, you should be able to articulate each Point in one sentence. Take time to reduce, clarify, and simplify the language of your Points so you are at the heart of the concept you want to get across.

Again, it's helpful for your listeners if you actually state your Point, followed by the Story and the Application. This gives them verbal markers to help them keep your concepts organized in their heads.

Story

Stories are the center point of any talk. They add flavor and interest to the concepts you are teaching. When I say "story," I mean any type of illustration that helps people to understand your message in an interesting way.

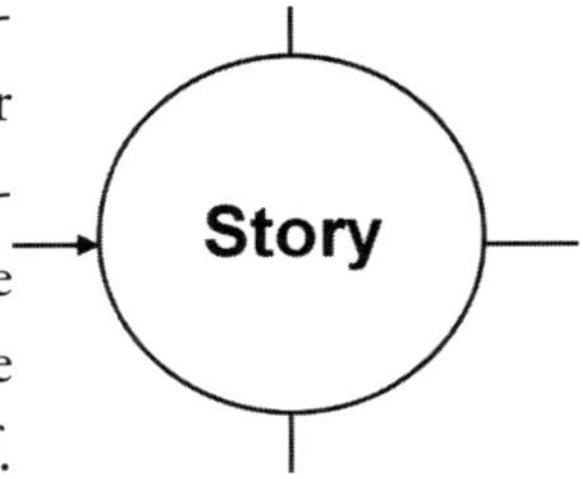

Stories make your talk memorable. They help to reduce difficult or complex subjects into easy-to-understand images. Well-crafted Stories are the pinnacle of teaching and were often used by the Savior himself. Think, for example, of His parable of the mustard seed in explaining the concept of faith, or the parable of the good Samaritan in teaching how we should treat one another.

The most powerful Stories will be those you draw from your own life. Why? As we learned with my Story about the apricot tree, when you have a personal, emotional connection with a story, the members of the congregation will feel a similar connection to it and to you. In Chapter Seven, you'll learn how to find original material for your Stories and how to hone and polish them until they sparkle.

Apply

In Chapter Four, we learned that people often listen to talks with an attitude of, "So what? How does this apply to me?" In this element, you tell your listeners why and how the concepts apply to their lives. This is your opportunity to explain the lesson learned in the Story and how it relates to your Point. Make it personal by showing how it will specifically benefit your listeners and their families. You might also indicate a few steps they could take in order to Apply it in their lives.

This is where a particularly pertinent quote, poem, or scripture would be appropriate. I recommend that you use no more than two or three scriptures or quotes in your entire talk. This means you'll want to sift through all your materials until you find the ones that are the most poignant and applicable to what you are trying to say. This drives your Point home with much greater impact and avoids the tendency we all have for our minds to glaze over when the speaker is reading too many scriptures or quotes.

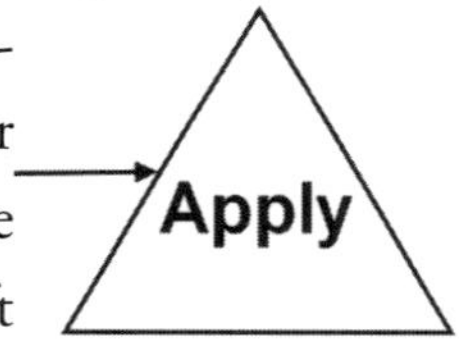

Summary

You opened your talk with a bang, presented your Anchor Statement and three major Points to support it, including Stories and ways to Apply each one. Now it's time to bring it all together so people will remember what you said. An easy way to do this is to review your Anchor Statement and then briefly touch on the three Points that support it. You can add a power punch to your Summary by reflecting back on your Opening and tying it back in to come full circle. You'll see an example of how to do this below.

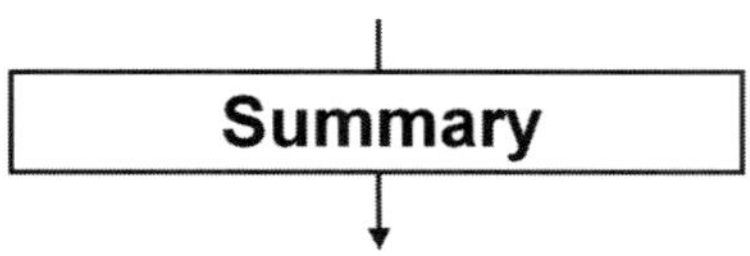

Testimony and Call to Action

Always conclude your talk with your Testimony and a Call to Action. This Testimony is different from what you might give in a fast and testimony meeting because it follows your talk and flows from the Summary of what you have said. In reality, your entire talk is an expression of your testimony; it's a statement and illustration of what you believe. As you bear a brief testimony of the specific principles you've discussed, it gives the Holy Ghost an important opportunity to bear witness to members of the congregation that the principles you have taught are true.

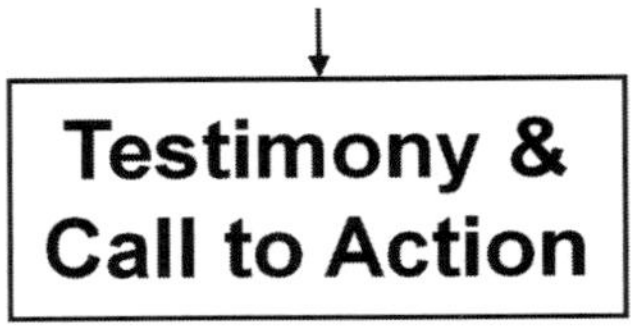

As a part of your testimony, you will also want to issue a Call to Action. This is where you encourage your listeners to do something about what you have said—to take action. The Apostle James encouraged, ". . . be ye doers of the word, and not hearers only."[21] Your Call to Action points everything that the members of the congregation have learned, felt, and experienced during your entire talk toward some kind of personal change, be it a change of heart or a change of practice.

Please see Chapter Seven for a more detailed discussion about Testimony and Call to Action.

Here's an Example

Now, let's look at an example of how this all fits together.

21 James 1:22

Let's say you Open your talk with this thought-provoking question:

> "As a mother of five children, I've often asked myself, 'Is it really worth the time, frustration, and energy it takes to hold family home evening?' Last Monday night started out badly, as it often does. John was asked to work late, and he arrived home tired. Sarah had a school project due, so she was a little cranky…"

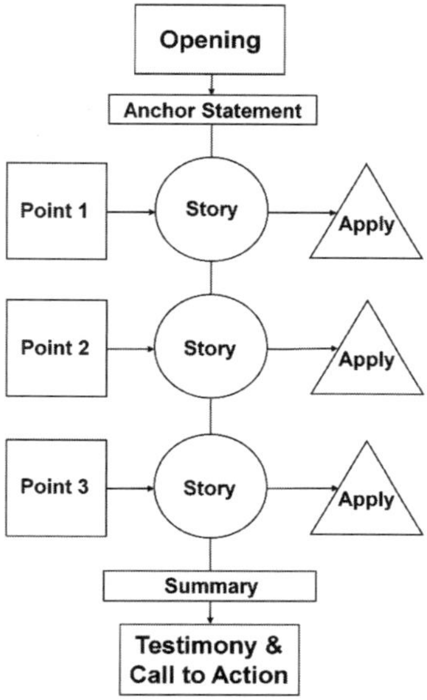

You get the idea. Now, you give your Anchor Statement, which might be something like:

> "With some prayer, planning, and heavenly help, family home evening can be an enjoyable and much-needed source of strength and protection for your family."

Your three Points might look something like this:

1. When you invite the Lord to your family home evening, it changes the spirit and tone of the experience.
2. Quality family home evenings require advanced planning.
3. Family home evening can fortify your family against the attacks of the world.

Each of these Points should be illustrated by an interesting

Story of something the family did or experienced, followed by ideas to Apply these concepts in our lives.

For instance, after giving point two above, the speaker might tell a Story about how after a particularly difficult family home evening, one child was assigned to give a part in the next one, and it turned out to be an unexpectedly spiritual experience for the family. The story would be followed by two or three ideas on how to Apply this concept by planning and preparing for a fantastic family home evening experience.

After giving all your Points with their corresponding Stories and Applications, you will give your Summary, which might sound something like this:

> "Brothers and sisters, I'm convinced that with some prayer, planning, and heavenly help, family home evening can be an enjoyable source of strength and protection for your family. We can 1) invite the Lord to our family home evenings to change the atmosphere; 2) have a quality experience by preparing and planning in advance; and 3) family home evening can be a source of strength to family members in a world that downplays the importance of the family.
>
> "At the beginning of my talk, I asked the question, 'Is it really worth the time, frustration, and energy it takes to hold family home evening every Monday night?' My answer is a resounding, yes! It is not only worth it, it can make all of the difference."

Notice how the Summary leads right into your Testimony and Call to Action:

"I testify that family home evening is an inspired program, received through holy prophets of God, to help us build and strengthen our families in the last days. May we give our family home evenings the planning, prayer, and priority necessary to bless each of our families, I pray, in the name of Jesus Christ, Amen."

Practice with Your Structure Chart

Now that you have filled out the structure chart and decided what you want to say for each element, you can use it to practice your talk. Start by laying out all your notes, along with your chart. Practice giving your talk from beginning to end using the structure chart as your guide, but referring to your notes as needed. As you practice, you'll find that you'll need fewer and fewer of your other notes and that you can remember most of your talk just by looking at the structure chart.

Notice that the chart is so visual you can immediately tell where you are in your talk by glancing down at it. Feel free to write trigger words or short notes by the elements on your chart to remind you what you want to say there.

Now, stand up with your chart and practice, visualizing yourself standing at the pulpit—calm, relaxed, and excited to share your message. Take your chart with you when you go for a walk. You'll be amazed at how walking while you practice can help solidify your message in your mind. Keep practicing until you feel comfortable. Pretty soon, you will know it so well that you can forget your notes altogether and simply use your structure chart to keep you on track. This allows you to focus on the congregation instead of worrying about what you are going to say.

Chapter 5
THE OPENING

How many times have you heard a talk begin like this?

"Uh, hi. Well, there I was, just sitting and minding my own business at Mutual, and then here comes Brother Bishopric and he sat down next to me and I didn't think much about it, but he started talking to me and we talked about the weather and school, but then he dropped the big question and asked me to talk in church and I was so mad that I came to Mutual and I went right over and told Joe about it and then Sam and they were like, 'Wow,' and I was like, 'Yeah,' and they all laughed at me, but then when I got home I told my mom about it and she was excited, and anyway, I started to think about the topic and so now I'm like really glad to be here to give this talk..."

I wrote this as if a youth were giving it, but I've heard just as many adults start this way, with a rambling narration of how they received the call to talk in church. We've probably all done this at one time or another. What we might not have realized is that we just wasted four minutes of our precious time saying nothing.

Start Boldly to Get Their Attention

Speaking experts tell us that we have less than two minutes to grab the audience's attention. If you can start boldly, letting the congregation know that you have something to say that will be interesting, informative, and uplifting, you will have significantly improved your entire talk. This is true because the way you begin your talk and the way you end your talk are more important than the entire balance of the talk put together.

Here is the first important rule about your opening:

Start strong to grab your listener's attention right away.

People have short attention spans. Commercials that used to last thirty seconds, or even a minute, now get the message across in only fifteen seconds. Your listeners are used to quick, flashy, entertaining messages. Is it any wonder that they start yawning if you're five minutes into your talk and you haven't really started yet? And if you lose your audience at the beginning, it's very hard to get them back later.

The purpose of the opening is to start boldly. Jump in and start, without any preamble or introduction. Avoid beating around the bush, telling jokes, apologizing, or telling how you received the call to talk. Just start.

Of course, there are instances when you need to briefly preface your remarks. If the person who spoke before you said something that relates directly to your topic, you might comment on that. If the Spirit prompts you to say something about the musical number or how much you love the ward, say it.

But in most cases, your opening will have more impact if you just start. If you are opening with a quote, for example, rather than saying, "I would like to start my talk with a quote," just give the quote. If your opening is a story, just start telling it. This indicates to your listeners that you have something to say and they'd better pay attention right off the bat.

The first two minutes are also when you are likely to feel the most nervous. A strong, well-crafted opening will do wonders to alleviate anxiety and set the tone for the rest of your comments.

Seven Ways to Open Your Talk

While there are limitless ways to start with a strong opening, they all fit into seven basic categories:

1) Story
2) Expressions of gratitude and love for the Saints
3) Amazing statistic or fact
4) Question
5) Foreshadowing
6) Bold statement
7) Quote

Below, we'll look at each of these openings in detail, along with actual examples of how they have been used in general conference and the scriptures. But first, let's look at the second foundational rule for your opening:

Your opening must be relevant to your topic and lead into the Anchor Statement of your talk.

Never open with something that doesn't contribute to the point of your talk. You may have found something exceptionally clever or funny, but if it doesn't relate, it's out of place and could actually detract. You'll see many excellent examples below of how to craft your opening so it naturally leads into your Anchor Statement.

Story

One of the best ways to open your talk is with an interesting story. It immediately grabs the attention of the congregation and leads them into your talk. Narrative stories are much easier to follow than abstract statements.

Don't announce that you're going to tell a story, just do it. The exception is when your lead-in gives some important information or sets the tone, such as:

"Let me tell you a story that's never been told."

"I'm going to tell you an amazing love story."

But in most cases, it's best to just start telling the story.

As we have mentioned before, your stories should be either original stories from your life, or at the very least, unique stories (that haven't been told repeatedly) that you can learn well enough to deliver confidently. One mistake we sometimes make is over-using stories that have meant something to us in the past, but often, these stories are also very familiar to everyone in the congregation.

For example, if we stand up and say, "I'm going to read a story that Elder Bednar told in the last conference," this signals to your listeners that 1) they've already heard it before, and 2) you are going to read it, so it won't have the same emotion and energy as when Elder Bednar originally gave it. You might as well say, "Please feel free to sleep through the next five minutes!"

Below are some sample openings, taken from actual talks by exceptional speakers in the Church, that begin with a story. Notice how one or two lines immediately draw you into the story so you want to hear what comes next.

> "A certain man planted a vineyard, and set an hedge about it, and...went into a far country."[22]

> "As a young boy I discovered amazing power in a small flashlight."[23]

> "In the 1960s, a professor at Stanford University began a modest experiment testing the willpower of four-year-old children. He placed before them a large marshmallow and then told them they could eat it right away or, if they waited for fifteen minutes, they could have two marshmallows."[24]

22 Jesus Christ, Mark 12:1

23 The Power of Light and Truth, Elder Robert R. Steuer, April 2008 Conference

24 Continue in Patience, Dieter F. Uchtdorf, Apr 2010 Conference

"When I was a young boy, one of our neighbors had a herd of dairy cows. One of his cows died, leaving a new born calf, which he gave to me. I took care of the calf, fed it, and raised it. The day my dad took it to the stockyards to be sold…"[25]

"Recently I was driving my car as drops of rain from a thunderstorm began to fall on the windshield. On the side of the road, an electronic sign displayed a timely warning…"[26]

"Behold there went out a sower to sow…"[27]

"A young couple, Lisa and John, moved into a new neighborhood. One morning while they were eating breakfast, Lisa looked out the window and watched her next-door neighbor hanging out her wash."[28]

"Recently I received a letter from a friend of over fifty years who is not a member of our church."[29]

"As a youth I visited the 1964 World's Fair in New York City."[30]

"I recently observed the birth of tiny Kate Elizabeth. After she entered this world…"[31]

25 The Best Investment, Elder Sheldon F. Child, April 2008 Conference
26 Watching with All Perseverance, David A. Bednar, Apr 2010 Conference
27 Jesus Christ, Mark 3:4
28 Charity Never Faileth, Thomas S. Monson, Oct 2010 Relief Society Conference
29 Agency: Essential to the Plan of Life, Robert D. Hales, Oct 2010 Conference
30 Reflections on a Consecrated Life, D. Todd Christofferson, Oct 2010 Conference
31 Stay on the Path, Rosemary M. Wixom, Oct 2010 Conference

Expressions of Gratitude and Love for the Saints

This is a wonderful way to begin your talk as it automatically establishes an emotional connection between you and the congregation, especially when you are specific and sincere. However, here again, it must follow the rule that it leads into the Anchor Statement. Watch how President Henry B. Eyring does this:

> "Brethren, I am grateful to be with you tonight. And I am humbled by what I know of your faithful priesthood service…"[32]

What do you think his talk will be about? Yes, you guessed it—it's on priesthood service.

Here's an example from Elder Holland. Notice how, little by little, he brings each segment of the congregation into the scope of his love. With this opening, he not only expresses his compassion for the Saints, but he establishes common ground individually with each listener:

> "Brothers and sisters, my Easter-season message today is intended for everyone, but it is directed in a special way to those who are alone or feel alone or, worse yet, feel abandoned. These might include those longing to be married, those who have lost a spouse, and those who have lost—or have never been blessed with—children. Our empathy embraces wives forsaken by their husbands,

32 Act in All Diligence, Henry B. Eyring, April 2010 Conference

> husbands whose wives have walked away, and children bereft of one or the other of their parents—or both. This group can find within its broad circumference a soldier far from home, a missionary in those first weeks of home sickness, or a father out of work, afraid the fear in his eyes will be visible to his family. In short it can include all of us at various times in our lives."[33]

Here's another opening by President Eyring. Notice how he masterfully weaves his message of love for the Saints into an introduction to his topic. See if you can guess what this talk will be about.

> "My beloved brothers and sisters, it is a joy to be gathered with you on this Sabbath morning. We live in many different circumstances. We will come from every nation and many ethnic backgrounds into the kingdom of God. And that prophesied gathering will accelerate. We see increased conflict between peoples in the world around us. Those divisions and differences could infect us."[34]

If you guessed unity, you are right again.

Interesting Statistic or Fact

Amazing statistics or interesting facts capture the interest of the listeners right away and give you a chance to introduce your Anchor Statement. As always, you must be able to relate the fact to your topic.

33 None Were with Him, Elder Jeffrey R. Holland, April 2009 Conference
34 Our Hearts Knit as One, President Henry B. Eyring. Oct 2008 Conference

Notice how President Gordon B. Hinckley grabs your attention with a statistic, then leads you naturally into his subject of the importance of fellowshipping:

> "Each year a substantial number of people become members of the Church, largely through missionary efforts. Last year there were 321,385 converts comprised of men, women, and children. This is a large enough number, and then some, in one single year to constitute 100 new stakes of Zion. One hundred new stakes per year. Think of it! This places upon each of us an urgent and pressing need to fellowship those who join our ranks."[35]

Here are some additional examples of starting with an interesting fact or statistic.

> "It's remarkable how much we can learn about life by studying nature. For example, scientists can look at the rings of trees and make educated guesses about climate and growing conditions hundreds and even thousands of years ago... During seasons when growing conditions are not ideal, trees slow down their growth and devote their energy to the basic elements necessary for survival."[36]

> "Wherever I am in the day or night, there is nearby a small container of olive oil."[37]

35 Converts and Young Men, Gordon B. Hinckley, April 1997 Conference
36 Of Things That Matter Most, Dieter F. Uchtdorf, Oct 2010 Conference
37 Be Ready, Henry B. Eyring, October 2009 Conference

"Suppose for a moment someone told you these three facts about a New Testament personality and nothing more: first, the Savior said of this man, "O thou of little faith"; second, this man, in a moment of anger, cut off an ear of the high priest's servant; and third, this man denied knowing who the Savior was on three occasions, even though he had walked with Him daily. If that is all you knew or focused upon, you might have thought this man a scoundrel or a no-good, but in the process you would have failed to come to know one of the greatest men who ever walked the earth: Peter the Apostle."[38]

Question

One of the most stimulating ways to begin a talk is with a question that makes your listeners think. Always the master teacher, Jesus often started His comments with questions.

Here are a few examples:

- "What think ye of Christ? whose son is he?"[39]
- "How can Satan cast out Satan?"[40]
- "Whom do men say that I am?"[41]
- "What was it that ye disputed among yourselves along the way?"[42]

Since you are speaking in church, your questions will be rhetorical. But they can still cause your audience to pause and reflect.

38 Joseph Smith—Prophet of the Restoration, Tad R. Callister, Oct 2009 Conference
39 Matthew 22:42
40 Mark 3:23
41 Mark 8:27
42 Mark 9:33

Watch how Elders Wirthlin and Scott do this in these openings:

> "Brethren and sisters, I would like to ask one very important question. What quality defines us best as members of The Church of Jesus Christ of Latter-day Saints? Today I would like to speak about the answer to this question."[43]

> "I wonder, brethren, how many of us seriously ponder the inestimable value of holding the Aaronic and Melchizedek Priesthoods."[44]

Questions logically lead to your Anchor Statement. You can also refer back to them throughout your talk and in your summary to bring your talk full circle. Here are a few more examples:

> "We have gathered together as one, we have taken upon us the name of Jesus Christ, and we are Christians. One of the questions we would ask: why then, if we have that love of the Savior, would someone want to be an antagonist or to attack us?"[45]

> "Since truth is the only meaningful foundation upon which we can make wise decisions, how then can one establish what is really true?"[46]

43 The Great Commandment, Elder Joseph B. Wirthlin, Oct 2007 Conference
44 Honor the Priesthood and Use It Well, Elder Richard G. Scott, Oct 2008 Conference
45 Christian Courage: The Price of Discipleship, Elder Robert D. Hales, Oct 2008 Conference
46 Truth: The Foundation of Correct Decisions, Elder Richard G. Scott, Oct 2007 Conference

Foreshadowing

This is a skill used often in movies or literature where something the main character does or says foreshadows something that will come later. It intrigues the audience into paying closer attention. It arouses curiosity. This technique can be used in your talk for the same purpose.

A foreshadowing opening might tell your listeners, "There is a story coming later," such as in this sentence which I used in a recent talk:

> "November 11, 1983 is a date that I will never forget. It started out as an ordinary day in the mission field. Little did we know the Lord was about to answer the prayer of two missionaries in a way we never would have expected."

Another way to use foreshadowing is to set up a problem and intimate that the listeners should watch for the solution to appear later, as in this example by Jay E. Jensen:

> "As a young elder I had been in the mission field about one year, and while reading scriptures and words of the latter-day Apostles about revelation and the Holy Ghost, I had a stunning awakening. I did not have a testimony of my own…"[47]

More examples of foreshadowing:

"I consider June 2, 1940, to be a very important day in

47 The Holy Ghost and Revelation, Jay E. Jensen, Oct 2010 Conference

> the history of my family. On this day my father was baptized into this Church."[48]

> "Many years ago, I observed a heartbreak—which became a tragedy."[49]

Bold Statement

Another way to open your talk is with a statement so bold that it attracts interest. This tells the congregation that you have big plans for the next few minutes and they should pay attention. They must be delivered with passion and sincerity. If you start with a bold claim, be sure that you can deliver what you promised.

Years ago, I remember Elder Bruce R. McConkie standing up in conference and delivering the following statement. He gave it with such power and confidence that I still remember it word for word to this day. He said:

> "I shall tell you how the keys of the kingdom operate, including from whence they came, where they now vest, and what their future is."[50]

Here are some more examples of openings that are bold statements:

> "No Father would send His children off to a distant, dangerous land for a lifetime of testing where Lucifer was

48 Because My Father Read the Book of Mormon, Elder Marcos A. Aidukaitis, Oct 2008 Conference
49 Turn to the Lord, Donald L. Hallstrom, Apr 2010 Conference
50 The Keys of the Kingdom, Bruce R. McConkie, May 1983 Conference

known to roam free without first providing them with a personal power of protection. He would also supply them with means to communicate with Him from Father to child and from child to Father."[51]

"You will need bravery and you will need boldness because you are enlisted in the Lord's army in the last dispensation. This is not a time of peace."[52]

"Verily verily I say unto thee, except a man be born of water and of the Spirit, he cannot enter into the kingdom of heaven."[53]

"My purpose tonight is to help you grow in your confidence that you can and will rise to the blessings of the oath and covenant of the priesthood. It is the magnitude of the possible consequences of that oath and covenant which may require a regular boost in your confidence."[54]

"I have been impressed to speak about God's love and God's commandments. My message is that God's universal and perfect love is shown in all the blessings of His gospel plan, including the fact that His choicest blessings are reserved for those who obey His laws."[55]

"We live in a most remarkable time—but a challenging time. The Lord has not left us alone in our quest to return to Him."[56]

51 Prayer and Promptings, Boyd K. Packer, Oct 2009 Conference
52 "Man Down!", Henry B. Eyring, April 2009 Conference
53 Jesus Christ, John 3:5
54 Faith and the Oath and Covenant of the Priesthood, Henry B. Eyring, April 2008 Conference
55 Love and Law, Dallin H. Oaks, Oct 2009 Conference
56 Never Leave Him, Neil L. Andersen, Oct 2010 Conference

Quote

If you have an interesting, thought-provoking quote that introduces your subject well, it can be an excellent way to begin your talk. It's even better if your quote is fresh and unique, not one that is oft quoted in the Church. Here are some examples of talks that start with a quote:

> "The Prophet Joseph Smith said: 'The building up of Zion is a cause that has interested the people of God in every age; it is a theme upon which prophets, priests and kings have dwelt with peculiar delight; they have looked forward with joyful anticipation to the day in which we live;"[57]

> "'Young men speak of the future because they have no past, and old men speak of the past because they have no future.' I am an old man, but I will speak to the young men of the Aaronic Priesthood about your future."[58]

Practice Your Opening

Once you have decided how you want to open your talk, you should write out your opening word for word so you can edit and sculpt it into a well-crafted, dynamic opening. Spend time practicing and rehearsing until you can give it without thinking. Most of all, practice looking people in the eye and starting with confidence and enthusiasm. You'll be amazed at what a difference it makes.

57 Come to Zion, Elder D. Todd Christofferson, Oct 2008 Conference
58 Counsel to Young Men, President Boyd K. Packer, April 2009 Conference

Chapter 6
THE POWER OF STORIES

The first time I spoke in church after we got married, I asked my wife, "How did I do?"

"It was…uh…fine," she replied.

"Fine?"

"Well, you could tell some stories to make it interesting," she said.

"I don't do stories in church," I remarked. "I'm a doctrinal speaker—like the General Authorities."

"General Authorities use lots of stories in their talks," she replied.

"No, they don't," I countered stubbornly.

Well, the next time general conference came, we decided to pay close attention so we could settle our difference of opinion. You guessed it—I lost. Big time. Church leaders know what the Savior knew two thousand years ago: stories are critical elements in any talk.

Why Stories Are Important

What conference talks do you remember best? Usually, they contain a central story that made them stick in your memory. You remember the story, and then the principle they were teaching is also brought to mind. As we discussed in Chapter Five, stories should be the central feature of every talk.

My friend, Patricia Fripp, is a highly sought-after executive speech coach and former president of the National Speaker's Association. She says:

> *People don't remember what you say, they remember the pictures they see when you speak.*

Stories paint those pictures. They add color and flavor to your talk. Stories are to a talk what pictures are to a book. They help you create a mental picture of the concepts you are learning.

Throughout the book, when I use the word "story," I include anything that illustrates the points of your talk in an interesting way. This could include examples, metaphors, parables, allegories, anecdotes, or actual stories.

Listen to President Dieter F. Uchtdorf describe his search for a compelling story to illustrate a particular talk.

> "I have known for a few months the message I want to give to you today. During that time, I have searched for a story that would illustrate what I want to say. I looked for

> a story about farming. I looked for a story about animals. In honor of Elder Scott, I looked for a story about nuclear engineering, and in honor of President Monson, one about raising pigeons.
>
> "In the end, one story kept coming back to me—a story that has been imprinted on my memory for many, many years. It isn't about farming, animals, nuclear engineering, or pigeons. It is as you might have guessed—about aviation. I call it 'The Story of the Light Bulb.'"[59]

We can learn two things from President Uchtdorf's comment. First, he felt so strongly that a story was critical to delivering his message that he searched for months to find just the right one. And second, he settled on something he is knowledgeable and passionate about—aviation.

In short, stories are important because:

1. they make your talk interesting and memorable
2. there is no better way to describe and clarify the complex
3. they paint mental pictures
4. they add color and flavor to your talk
5. they add variety by transporting your audience to a different place and time
6. they establish an emotional connection with your listeners

59 We Are Doing a Great Work and Cannot Come Down, Dieter F. Uchtdorf, April 2009 Conference

Use Your Own Original Stories

One of the biggest complaints I heard when compiling the Top 10 List of Mistakes People Make Speaking in Church was that talks are boring. What makes a talk boring? There are four main causes of a boring talk:

1. The material is strictly intellectual; there is no emotional or spiritual connection.
2. The material lacks interest and variety.
3. The material is worn out and over-used; we've heard it all before.
4. The speaker's delivery is dry and uninteresting.

We'll talk about delivery in Chapter Nine, but the first three causes of a boring talk can be instantly solved with well-told, original stories. Personal stories are fresh and unique, and the more honest and genuine you are, the better the emotional connection.

Stories don't necessarily have to be about you to be unique. They could be about anyone or anything. The important thing is that you are the author of the story and you have an emotional connection to the story. However, the most compelling stories will always be personal.

The good news is that original stories are easy to come up with because they are all around you, waiting to be discovered.

We All Tell Stories

We tell stories in the hallway at church, around the water fountain at work, at the dinner table, or socializing with friends. Often we use our best stories to entertain our friends and don't even think to use them in our talks. If you have told a story to two or more people, it's potential material for a talk.

Years ago, I overheard one of the young women in our ward telling her friends an animated story in the halls at church. The way she told it was dynamic, interesting, and fun. It went something like this:

As she was putting her books in her locker at school, a boy went up to some friends nearby and started talking with a loud voice. He told of some bizarre things that he and his friends had done, punctuating his remarks with profanity. After a while, she realized that this conversation was meant to impress her. A few minutes later, he came over and asked her out.

This young woman's final comment to her friends was, "Yeah, like I would go out with someone who talked like that. Not!"

It was a fantastic story, with a built-in gospel message.

Several weeks later, that same young woman was asked to speak in sacrament meeting. She got up, and in a monotone voice, began: "Today – I – will – talk – about – faith. Faith – is – the – first – principle – of – the – gospel…"

How sad that this dynamic young woman was never

taught how to use personal stories and enthusiasm when speaking in church. It could have been a vibrant and interesting talk—one that every young man should hear. Instead, she simply spoke as she had heard so many other youth before her.

Great Stories Can Come from the Simplest Things

Jesus told His stories about simple, everyday tasks like sweeping the floor, tending sheep, building a tower, and planting seeds; He compared everyday objects such as seeds, water, bread, money, and even the weather to gospel themes. You, too, can learn to see a story in everyday situations—it's an art that can be developed. Don't ever feel that your stories are not dynamic or miraculous enough to be used in a talk. The original idea is not as important as how you tell it and relate it to the gospel. Later in this chapter, you'll learn how to turn an ordinary story into a great illustration.

Once I was assigned to give a talk on developing Christlike attributes. I thought about the members of our ward who already embody many of the attributes of Christ, but don't realize it. They reminded me of the story in the Book of Mormon about the Lamanites, of whom the Lord said that they received the Holy Ghost, but they knew it not.[60] I wanted a story to illustrate this concept. I prayed for guidance and then thought, "What stories have I been telling lately?"

The week before, I had taken my son on a winter camp with the Scouts. Something interesting happened, and I had

60 3 Nephi 9:20

recounted it to several people. Here's the story that developed from that simple experience:

One February, I went with my twelve-year-old son, Clyde, on a winter Scout camp. Clyde and his friend were determined to build and sleep in a snow cave. So, from the moment we arrived at the campsite, they were digging and shaping the perfect snow cave.

The rest of us were sleeping in tents and we encouraged our boys to do the same, but they wouldn't hear of it. "We're sleeping in the snow cave!" they insisted. By bed time, with some help from the adults, the cave was eight-feet square and about two-and-a-half-feet high. I started to worry that it would collapse during the night. We made the boys promise to sleep with their heads toward the door so if it caved in, we could easily rescue them.

We got them settled and went to bed. Just as my head hit the pillow, it started to rain—softly at first, but then harder until it became a downpour. I began to worrying about what all that rain would do to the snow cave. "Could the ceiling become so water-logged that it might collapse?" I wondered.

I prayed that the rain would stop, or turn to snow, so our sons would be safe, but the rain didn't stop. I worried and fretted, in and out of sleep. Minute followed minute, hour after hour, and the rain continued. I began praying that if the rain wasn't going to stop, that the Lord would shore up the walls and ceiling of the snow cave so it could stand strong and protect our boys.

Finally about 3 a.m., I got up and looked out of the tent. To my amazement, I saw that it hadn't been raining at all. It was a fine, granular snow that sounded just like rain on the roof of the tent. All the while, as I had been worrying that the rain would undermine the snow cave, the snow was actually fortifying and strengthening it.

We all have challenges in our lives that we believe will be our breaking point. "This is the one that will destroy my faith and my family," we say. Meanwhile, through these difficult experiences, the Lord is quietly and steadily building our faith, strengthening our resolve, and developing us into more Christ-like Saints.

Don't Be the Hero of Your Stories

Avoid stories where you are the hero, where you did every thing perfectly and others fell short. These tend to alienate the audience and make you seem "holier than thou."

I once heard a wise, respected member of our ward begin a story with this statement: "When I was in school, I had a really hard time learning." When he admitted this, he automatically endeared himself to everyone in the congregation. After all, who didn't have difficulty in school at one time or another? As a congregation, we were encouraged because, as I said, he was an intelligent and respected member of the ward. We also felt totally connected with him because you could feel his honesty as he shared what to him was not a proud moment.

Imagine how different the connection would have been if this man got up and said, "When I was in school, everything was easy for me, and I always got straight A's." I'm not feeling a lot of connection—how about you?

Let the congregation know that you didn't always have all the answers and that you are still learning right along with them. I'm not saying you should get up and start confessing your sins—you shouldn't. But you'll find that the stories that have the greatest impact are those where you made a mistake or discovered a weakness and learned a valuable lesson. Select examples where someone else does the right thing. Stories go over much better when you are taking the brunt of the story, rather than being the hero.

Here's an experience that happened to me as a young man. Notice that I bear the brunt of the story and my father is the hero.

> When I was about seventeen years old, my family went on a vacation, but I stayed home because I had to work.
>
> On Friday, some friends and I wanted to go to Bear Lake to meet some more friends and go waterskiing. My parents weren't due back until Saturday afternoon and there was no way to get hold of them (this was way before cell phones). It seemed harmless and I figured we would be back before my family returned home anyway, so I borrowed Dad's car and we drove to the lake.
>
> We had so much fun waterskiing that evening that we got up early the next morning and skied for a couple more hours before heading home.
>
> I was exhausted as we drove home, and sure enough, I fell asleep at the wheel while driving down Parley's Canyon. The car picked up speed and slammed into an other car from the rear. We hit with such force that the bumpers locked and we veered back and forth in unison

(you might call it synchronized crashing) before coming to a stop at the side of the road. Fortunately, no one was seriously injured, but the cars were demolished.

It was a disaster!

My first thought was, "My dad is going to kill me." The other driver used the police radio to call a tow truck, but I decided that if I pulled some of the twisted metal away from the tire, I could drive it home. What a sight I was, nursing a little red squished Honda home with the front completely crushed. I remember naively thinking, "If I can just get home before my parents do, maybe I can take it to a shop and get it fixed so no one will notice."

But as I rounded the corner, I knew I was in trouble. There was the family van in the driveway. I parked the car down the street, with the front end hidden behind some big bushes, and went in the house. Everyone was excitedly talking about their trip and it took me about ten minutes to bring myself to say, "Uh, Dad, I had a little accident while you were gone. I may have put a tiny dent in the car."

He said, "Let's take a look." So out we went, the whole family, to look at the car. My younger sisters ran on ahead and came running back, yelling, "It's smashed—it's all smashed!"

My father looked at the car for what seemed like a long time. "What happened?" he finally asked.

I told him the story and added, "You'll probably be getting a call from the guy that I hit! I'm so sorry."

After making sure no one was injured, he paused for a while, then said, "Well, let's get it fixed."

That's all.

I was ready for yelling; I was prepared for a lecture. But nothing prepared me for the grace and mercy I felt that day from my father.

I think that because of this experience with my father, I can somehow comprehend the grace and mercy that we all receive from Jesus Christ. Knowing that we would make terrible mistakes, He suffered and died for us in advance so that when we came to Him with a broken heart, He could extend mercy and grace to us.

Ideas for Original Stories

Original stories are all around you. The following list is filled with ideas you can use to discover stories from your own life, and those around you, that you can use in your talks. This list could be one of the most valuable things in this book. I'm convinced that if you will use these tips, purposefully and prayerfully, you will come up with numerous stories you can polish and utilize as you speak.

1. Think about humorous or interesting stories you have been recounting to friends lately. How could they illustrate a gospel principle?
2. What was your most embarrassing moment? What did you learn that could illustrate a gospel principle?
3. Think of experiences that happened to you as a child. What did you like to do for fun? What is the funniest story you remember from your childhood? What did you think was interesting? Boring?
4. What was the craziest thing that ever happened to you at church? School? Your job?
5. Think of a story you have told over and over about your children or spouse.

6. What happened at Scout camp, Young Women's camp, EFY, etc. that was memorable for you or taught you a lesson?
7. Think of times when the Lord took over and taught you something through an experience or trial that you could never have learned any other way.
8. Think of everyday tasks you do that might be related to a gospel topic.
9. Write down names of people who have influenced you. What did you learn from them? How did you learn it? What stories come to mind?
10. Ponder how you gained a testimony of the principle you've been assigned to talk about. What happened to help you gain this testimony?
11. Think of principles of the gospel that used to be difficult for you, but are now easier. What happened to make the difference?
12. Build a story around an interesting incident in your life, no matter how trivial, that you can relate to a gospel theme.
13. Interview people who will be in the congregation when you talk. Why do they go to church? How did they gain a testimony of this principle? What insights can they give you?
14. How did you learn about this principle as a child? Think of experiences where the Lord was teaching you, but you didn't realize it at the time.
15. How did you develop your character? What happened to form your beliefs?
16. When do you remember first being aware of the gospel principle that you are speaking about? Where were you? What happened?

17. Sit around a table with friends and a voice recorder. Tell stories that you love to tell about your life. Ask each other questions, as you would if you were out to dinner or at a party. Often, your best stories are those you use to entertain your friends.
18. Interview people about their lives. Talk to elderly people as well as young Primary children. The key to uncovering interesting stories is asking the right questions. Remember to write down and quote their exact dialogue in your stories.
19. What experiences have affected you the most emotionally? Why? What happened?
20. What unrelated personal experience or story could illustrate this principle?
21. Think of people you know who perfectly represent the principle you are talking about. Did they always embody this principle? If not, how did they develop it?
22. Read your journal. You'll be amazed at how many great stories you can get from a diary, baby book, or mission journal.
23. Think about a day in the life of a missionary, bishop, parent, home teacher, or Primary child.
24. What scripture story comes to mind when you think about this principle?
25. Reflect back on the experiences you have had in your life. Are there experiences that didn't mean much to you at the time, but have gained more meaning or relevance as you look back?
26. Search your family history for interesting things that happened to your ancestors.
27. Keep a note pad with you and write down memorable events as they happen to you. Record as much detail

as you can, including actual dialogue. We've all had the experience of seeing or experiencing something and thinking that it could apply to a gospel principle, but can we remember them later? Not unless we've written them down. Get a file folder at home labeled "stories" and place these hand-written notes in them. Then, when you are asked to give a talk, you can go to this folder and find a treasure trove of interesting ways to illustrate your points.

Remember, original content is everywhere, all around you. As you consider these suggestions, seek for the Spirit, and pay attention, you will find plenty of ideas for great stories.

What about Scripture Stories?

What about stories from the scriptures? They're certainly not original, but don't they make good material for a talk?

Yes, of course they do. However, there are two ways to tell a scripture story. One is to stand up and say, "I'll now read a story from the scriptures."

A better way is to learn the story, study its background, characters, and meaning, then tell the complete story in your own words, adding what it means to you personally. You can take a story from the scriptures and make it unique by fleshing it out and adding your personal connection to the story. When you do this, it becomes original in the sense that no one else tells it like you do.

General Authorities often do this in conference. They take a story from the scriptures and give it life by putting it in context, adding background to the characters, and personalizing the message. In this way, they are able to teach by the Spirit: intellectually, spiritually, and emotionally. Watch how skillfully Elder David B. Haight does this:

> "One day the Savior entered a village where there were ten lepers. Now, those of us who have grown up in the last few years know very little about lepers. Leprosy was a terrible, dreaded disease anciently.
>
> "These ten lepers came to the Savior and said, 'Master, have mercy upon us; have mercy upon us who have that terrible ailment of leprosy.' And He said to the ten lepers, 'Go visit your priest, and he will take care of you'—which they did. They went to see their priests, and they were cleansed, all ten of them.
>
> "A short time later, one of them returned to the Savior and fell on his face and his hands and his knees, thanking the Savior for blessing him and making him well from that terrible disease. And the Savior said to that one man: 'Weren't there ten? What has happened to the other nine? Where are they?'
>
> "As I've read that story again and again, it's made a great impression upon me. How would you like to be part of the 'nine society?' Wouldn't that be something—to be numbered among those who failed to return and acknowl edge the Savior for the blessings He had given them? Only one returned."[61]

61 Were There Not Ten Cleansed?, David B. Haight, Oct 2002 Conference (Compare with Luke 17:11–19)

Elements of a Good Story

Now that you have some ideas for stories you could tell, let's look at the elements you should include as you craft your story. All great stories have the following common elements. They must:

1. Be interesting and concise
2. Have real characters
3. Use dialogue
4. Transport you to a different place or time
5. Create pictures in your mind
6. Resonate with the audience so they can put themselves inside the story

Jesus was the master storyteller. His teachings are filled with parables, examples, and metaphors. I challenge you to read any of His parables without having a picture immediately appear in your mind. Even His most simple examples are easy to visualize.

Let's try one together:

> "…what woman having ten pieces of silver, if she lose one piece, doth not light a candle, and sweep the house, and seek diligently till she find it? And when she hath found it, she calleth her friends and her neighbours together, saying, 'Rejoice with me; for I have found the piece which I had lost.' Likewise, I say unto you, there is joy in the presence of the angels of God over one sinner that repenteth."[62]

62 Luke 15:8-10

How many of us have ever lost anything and searched everywhere trying to find it? We all have. Can't you actually see the woman scouring the house, shining her light everywhere and sweeping every corner of her house until she found the lost money? Can't you visualize her calling her friends and neighbors and celebrating? I think we all can. It is a powerful visual image, portrayed in just a few lines.

This simple example has all the elements of a great story: interest (who isn't interested in money), characters (the woman reminds me of my mother), dialogue (notice Jesus actually quotes what the woman says), it transports us to a different time and place (we are suddenly in Jerusalem with this woman), mental pictures (we can see her searching), and a personal emotional connection (we've all searched or something that was lost).

Polishing Your Stories—How to Make a Good Story Great

We all tell stories, but we seldom take the time to think about *how* we tell them and to work on the delivery so they're interesting instead of rambling.

You may have heard someone say, "That story gets better every time you tell it!" Sometimes they are implying that you are changing the facts or embellishing the story.

Not necessarily.

Stories get better with each telling because we tell it better each time. We organize the facts, we sculpt and clarify our words; we flesh out the characters; we use voice inflection and distinctive pauses; and we deliver it with more poise and enthusiasm. In short, we polish the story.

Let's look at some simple ways to improve your stories.

Write Out Your Stories

Once you have found a story you would like to use, I encourage you to write it out word for word.

You might think, "I know this story well, and I can tell it much better than I can write it out." That may be true, but I still encourage you to write it. If it's difficult for you to type or write, you could record the story and have someone transcribe it for you.

You'll use this written copy to help you to polish and practice. You should never read it at the pulpit. Stories should always be told in your own words while you look people in the eye.

Setting

Stories should transport the listener to a different time and place. You can do this by inserting descriptive word-pictures into your story. Watch as Elder L. Whitney Clayton masterfully transports us to a different time and place in just two short sentences:

> "Many years ago I walked at dawn through the narrow cobblestone streets of Cusco, Peru, high in the Andes Mountains. I saw a man from a local indigenous group walking down one of the streets."[63]

What did we learn about the setting of the story in those two sentences?

- The story happened many years ago
- It takes place at dawn
- In Cusco, Peru
- Which is high in the Andes Mountains
- The old city streets are narrow and paved with cobblestone
- Native people are walking up and down the streets

Notice how it paints a clear picture in your mind. Can you see it? Can you imagine that you are there, squinting in the early morning light as you stroll down the narrow cobblestone road? I can.

Be Accurate and Specific

Polishing a story *never* means altering the facts. In fact, the truer you can be to the details, the better your story will be. It's a good idea to verify the specifics of your story with another person who was there or to consult original sources

63 That Your Burdens May Be Light, L. Whitney Clayton, October 2009 Conference

such as your journal to make sure you are accurately reflecting what happened. The more honest and genuine you can be, the more your story will help you to connect with your listeners while you illustrate your points.

Be specific about details to add credibility and appeal to your stories. For example, instead of saying "There was a whole lot of snow," be specific and say "The snow was four feet, three inches deep" or "Snow drifts reached to the second-story window."

Sequence

One way to make your story more interesting is to change the sequence of how you tell it. For example, instead of starting at the beginning and telling the story sequentially, you might start at the climax and work backwards.

Or you could start in the middle.

Here's an example of a personal story from an event in my own family history. Notice how it starts in the middle of the timeline for a little dramatic effect.

> Over 150 years ago, somewhere in the wild plains of the west, a young mother of three lay sleeping in the tall golden grass. Her blistered feet dangled lazily in a shallow stream. A dusty wagon trail snaked through the grass not far from where she rested. There was no one else in sight for miles around.
>
> Suddenly, Martha jerked awake.
>
> "Where am I?" she thought. "How long was I asleep?"
>
> She turned around and saw to her dismay that the

wagon train had left. They must not have seen her wander ff to bathe her tired feet in the cool stream when they stopped for lunch.

"And now they've left without me," Martha cried to herself. She had no idea where she was and the wagons were out of sight, so she must have been asleep for at least two hours. Completely alone and becoming more and more frightened, she prayed that somehow she would be able to get back to the group and safety. She jumped up and started following the wagon tracks, walking as fast as she could, hoping she could catch up.

She was overcome with despair when she came to the Platte River crossing. She took off her shoes and started to wade, hoping and praying she could cross safely, but the current was too swift and deep. She turned back, dejected, and sat down on the side of the bank. Martha knew that alone on the plains, without shelter or protection, she stood little chance against wild animals after dark.

"Will I ever see my William and my little children alive again?" she sobbed as she prayed for help.

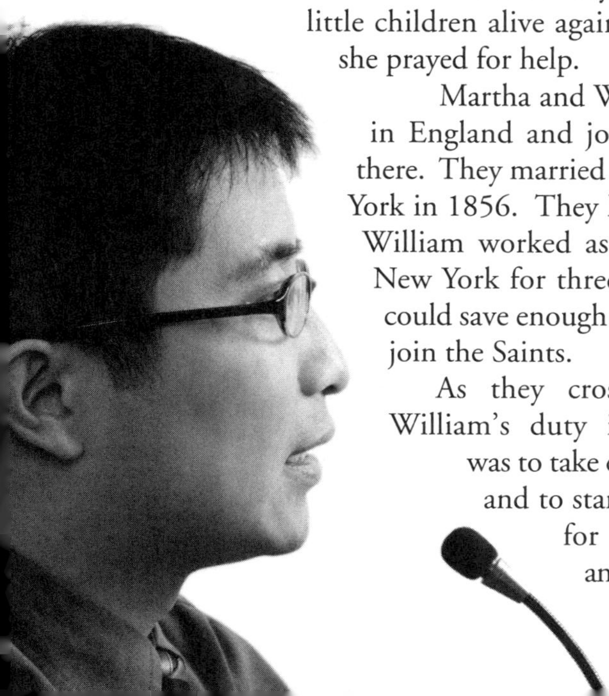

Martha and William were born in England and joined the Church there. They married and came to New York in 1856. They had no money, so William worked as a blacksmith in New York for three years until they could save enough to come west and join the Saints.

As they crossed the plains, William's duty in the company was to take care of the wagons and to stand watch at night for Indians or wild animals. Martha was in charge of cooking and looking after the children. Since the wagons were reserved for carrying supplies, both had to walk most of the thousand miles to Utah.

That day at lunch, Martha's feet had been so tired and blistered from walking that she felt like she just had to sit down by a stream of water to wash them off and rest for a moment. It had felt so good that she lay down by the stream…and fell asleep.

Now she was lost and stranded.

After a long while, sitting by the river, it seemed to Martha that her prayers were answered as she saw two horsemen, not part of their group, coming across the river from the opposite direction. They shouted a warning, "If you try to cross, you'll certainly drown."

As they came nearer, they began teasing her about being left behind. She was already so distracted she began to cry and prayed more than ever in her heart. The men apologized for teasing her and offered to give her a ride across the river.

Martha consented to climb on one of the horses and held on very tight. She was afraid that if she fell off in the middle of the treacherous stream, she would never see her husband or children again. Before they got to the other side, she could only see the top of the horse's head and the water came up beyond her arm pits. They finally landed her on the other side of the river and told her she would find the wagon train straight ahead.

It was beginning to get dark, and as she hurried to catch up, she could barely see, in the far distance, the company going around the mountain ahead.

It was some time before William discovered that Martha was missing. He immediately set out back toward the river to find her, worried that she had been injured or killed along the way. Finally, he spotted her, threw his arms around her, and they cried for joy that she was safe and alive.

Like Martha, we all have roadblocks and challenges which block our forward progress. We wonder if we will make it through the trials of life so we can see our family again in the eternities. When these moments of discouragement and despair come to me, I think about my great-great-grandmother, Martha Derricott: alone, stranded in the wilderness, trying to cross the Platte River, wondering whether she would live to see her family again. I know that just as the Lord helped her to cross the river and return safely to her family, He will also help me to overcome my obstacles and return safely to Him.

Add Background and Dialogue to Make Your Characters Real

Add appropriate details to flesh out your characters so the congregation can relate to them. Who are they? What is their background? What can help your listeners understand why they did what they did in your story?

In my story above, notice how a few lines of background make Martha and William into real people we can identify with.

Dialogue also makes them more real. In this case, I read the family history accounts about what Martha was thinking and feeling at the time and restated these thoughts as actual internal dialogue in the story. If you are telling something you experienced yourself, try to remember what people actually said and include it in your story. Instead of reporting on what someone said, as in:

> As we rounded the corner, Elder James felt impressed that we should stop at the blue house on the left.

Give the actual dialogue:

> As we rounded the corner, Elder James suddenly yelled, "Stop!" I brought my bike to a wobbly halt as he said, "Let's go to this blue house. I feel strongly that we should stop here."

Notice how dialogue makes the narration sparkle and brings the characters to life? Dialogue always makes a story more interesting and engaging.

Boost the Emotional Connection

Choose stories that mean something to you personally and elicit poignant feelings. Try to tell the story from the point of view of your listeners so they are inside the story. Make them feel involved and important.

Your stories don't necessarily have to be dramatic or miraculous in order to connect emotionally. Even trivial stories like the story of the apricot tree that I told in Chapter Three can create a deep emotional connection with your listeners. Much of the emotion is in the speaker's connection to the story. No one can tell your stories with the same emotion as you can tell them. Even if you read someone else's story word for word, you will never capture the emotion as well as they can.

In the pioneer story above, Martha Derricott is my great-great-grandmother. If she hadn't made it back to her family in safety, my great-grandmother would never have been born—and neither would I. Do I have an emotional connection? You bet.

As we learned in Chapter Three, make sure the tone of your story is in harmony with the upbeat, joyful message of the gospel. If your stories have some sad or tender moments, that's fine. Just make sure that the story ends on a positive and faith-promoting note.

Few members of the Church will forget the moving story President Monson related in April conference 2009. He told of a German woman in WWII who was forced to undertake a journey of over a thousand miles on foot, in winter, with four young children. He recounted the hardships and heartache of this faithful woman as one by one, her dear children died from exposure and hunger and she dug their shallow graves with the only instrument she had—a tablespoon. It was a heart-wrenching story. He then told of the comfort and peace that heaven bestowed on this sister in her darkest hour and the powerful testimony she bore upon reaching her destination, stating that "of all the ailing people in her saddened land, she was one of the happiest because she knew that God lived, that Jesus is the Christ, and that He died and was resurrected so that we might live again."[64]

President Monson characterized this story as being about

64 Be of Good Cheer, Thomas S. Monson, April 2009 Conference

"one who persevered and ultimately prevailed, despite overwhelmingly difficult circumstances." Thus, a sad tale became a story about the blessing of having the gospel in our lives. What was President Monson's overall message? "Be of good cheer. The future is as bright as your faith."

Refine Your Language

Now that you're sure you have all the pieces you want in your story, it's time to hone, polish, chisel, and rewrite. Here are some ideas:

1. Look for words that are vague or unclear and replace them with crisp language that better articulates your meaning.
2. Use words that create visual pictures.
3. Try to reduce the number of words it takes to tell the story.
4. Eliminate extraneous details or words that don't contribute to the story. We all like to talk about ourselves, but this is not the time to drone on about things that aren't relevant.
5. Try to put the most important word at the end of the sentence or phrase in order to give it more emphasis. Instead of saying, "Every night I study my scriptures before I go to bed," you might say, "Every night before I go to bed, I study my scriptures." This puts the emphasis on "scriptures" rather than "bed."

As you refine the language of your talk, you might ask a trusted friend or family member to read through your story and ask questions about what they don't understand. This helps you discover parts that may need additional clarification. Your friends may also have suggestions on better ways to present your story for greater impact.

The more you can clarify, reduce, and crystallize your stories, the more crisp and forceful they will be at illustrating your points, and the more memorable your talk will be.

As in all things, the Savior is the perfect example. He spent many hours alone in prayer and preparation for His ministry.[65] I believe some of that solitary time was spent organizing and preparing how He would teach the truths of the gospel to the people. Consider the parables of Jesus, for example. Each word and phrase is so packed with meaning that a volume of teaching occurs in just a few lines. It's reasonable to suppose that these stories were practiced, polished, improved, and rehearsed by the Savior well in advance of their being presented in public.

What is the Gospel Connection?

Don't forget that the purpose of your story is to relate a gospel message. This should be uppermost in your mind. The sentence that connects your story to the point you're trying to illustrate is just as important as the rest of the story. Make sure it, too, is well crafted and clearly stated.

65 See Matthew 14:31; Luke 4:1, 5:16; Mark 1:35; John 6:15

Practice and Rehearse

After you are satisfied with the story, read it over and over until you can tell the improved version naturally in your own words. Practice telling the story to yourself and to others. If parts are humorous or suspenseful, practice your delivery so your timing is perfect. The more time you take to practice and rehearse your stories, the more natural and unstudied they will appear, and the more impact they will have. We'll learn more about delivery techniques in Chapter Nine.

Save Your Stories

When you're finished with your talk, file and save these written copies of your stories so you'll remember them later. Many times, as I have referred back to notes of a talk I gave several years earlier, I see a notation such as "Tell the story about John." Unfortunately, I can't remember what story it is or even which John the story is about! A written copy expands your memory so you can go back and refer to it later.

You may even use the same story to illustrate a different point in a later talk to a different congregation.

These written stories can also become a treasured part of your family history that will be read and cherished by your children and grandchildren for generations to come.

Is It Worth It?

At this point, you might be saying, "This seems like a lot of work just to tell a simple story!"

You're right, it is. But it's also the number one thing that will help you to connect with the audience. Stories are the center point of your talk. They take the most work, but they also have the greatest impact.

Chapter 7
Testimony and Call to Action

The most important part of your talk, of course, is how you conclude. In Part I of this chapter, you'll learn how to finish your talk with a brief testimony of the principles discussed and a Call to Action. In Part II, we'll discuss bearing a stand-alone testimony, as you would in a fast and testimony meeting.

Part I: Concluding Your Talk

Call to Action

When I first began writing this book, I simply put "testimony" in this final slot because I was always taught that you should conclude your talk with a testimony. I was half right. Then I began watching great speakers in the Church. I read and listened to hundreds of conference talks by General Authorities. And I discovered something unexpected. Many don't close with a testimony at all!

I'm not saying that we don't get their testimony. Their entire talk is, in fact, an expression of their testimony of the principle of the gospel they are teaching. But I was interested to learn that General Authorities almost always end their talks with a Call to Action: a challenge or expression of hope that we will act on the things we have been taught. Here are some examples of talks that end this way:

> "**May we** consecrate ourselves as sons and daughters of God, 'that when he shall appear we shall be like him, for we shall see him as he is; that we may have this hope,' I pray in the name of Jesus Christ, amen."[66]

> "**Let us** simplify our lives a little. Let us make the changes necessary to refocus our lives on the sublime beauty of the simple, humble path of Christian discipleship—the path that leads always toward a life of meaning, gladness, and peace. For this I pray, as I leave you my blessing, in the sacred name of Jesus Christ, amen."[67]

> "**May we** understand and live in thanksgiving for the priceless gifts that come to us as sons and daughters of a loving Heavenly Father and for the promise of that bright day when we shall all rise triumphant from the grave. That we may always know that no matter how dark our Friday, Sunday will come is my prayer, in the name of Jesus Christ, amen."[68]

The Call to Action focuses everything that your listeners have learned, felt, and experienced during your talk into a desire to change. This is where you encourage them to not just listen and learn, but to do. It is the culmination of your effort as a speaker.

66 Reflections on a Consecrated Life, D. Todd Christofferson, Nov 2010 Conference
67 Of Things That Matter Most, Dieter F. Uchtdorf, Nov 2010 Conference
68 Sunday Will Come, Joseph B. Wirthlin, Oct 2006 Conference

The Call to Action often includes phrases such as: "let us," "may we," and "I pray." Here are some additional examples of each:

> "He gave His life to redeem mankind. Surely we can accept responsibility for those He entrusts to our care. Brethren, **let us** be men, even as He is. In the name of Jesus Christ, amen."[69]

> "I testify that my witness of these things is true and that the heavens are open to all who seek the same confirmation. Through the Holy Spirit of Truth, **may we** all know "the only true God, and Jesus Christ, whom [He has] sent." Then **may we** live Their teachings and be true Christians in deed, as well as in word, I pray in the name of Jesus Christ, amen."[70]

> "**It is my prayer** that we will recognize and root out un righteous pride in our hearts and that we will replace it with 'righteousness, godliness, faith, love, patience, [and] meekness.' In the sacred name of Jesus Christ, amen."[71]

Let's watch as President Thomas S. Monson uses all three of these phrases in his closing statement at the priesthood session of the October 2006 conference:

> "Brethren, **let us** learn our duties. **Let us** ever be worthy to perform those duties and, in so doing, follow in the footsteps of the Master. When to Him came the call of duty, He answered, "Father, thy will be done, and the

69 Let Us Be Men, D. Todd Christofferson, Oct 2006 Conference
70 The Only True God and Jesus Christ Whom He Hath Sent, Jeffrey R. Holland, Oct 2007 Conference
71 Pride and the Priesthood, Dieter F. Uchtdorf, Nov 2010 Conference

> glory be thine forever." **May we** do likewise, **I pray** humbly, in the name of Jesus Christ the Lord, amen."[72]

Another way to conclude with a Call to Action is by issuing a challenge with promise.

Listen to Elder L. Tom Perry challenge the youth of the Aaronic Priesthood.

> "Young men, **I challenge you** to build your lives on a foundation of truth and righteousness… **I also challenge you** to determine today that you will honor this great blessing and prepare to advance in each office of the Aaronic Priesthood—deacon, teacher, and priest… **I promise you** if you will prepare to receive His holy priesthood, He will literally pour out blessings upon your heads. This witness I leave with you in the name of our Lord and Savior, even Jesus the Christ, amen."[73]

We all hope people will like our talks—that they will be able to stay awake and perhaps even learn something. But when we take it a level higher, we hope that our talks can be not just enjoyable, but that they will motivate people to action. My friend and mentor, Mark Benson, would often quote the old saying, "The test of a preacher is not that people go away saying, 'what a great sermon,' but 'I will do something!'" That is the highest level of achievement for any teacher or speaker.

72 True to Our Priesthood Trust, Thomas S. Monson, Oct 2006 Conference
73 The Priesthood of Aaron, L. Tom Perry, October 2010 Conference

Testimony

When you conclude your talk, since you have spoken about a specific principle of the gospel, it is appropriate that you bear your testimony of that principle. This gives the Holy Ghost one last opportunity to testify that this principle is true and to whisper personalized inspiration to individuals in the congregation as to how they could apply it in their lives.

Occasionally we hear members in sacrament meeting finish their talk and then shift gears by saying, "I will now bear my testimony"—as if the testimony had nothing to do with the preceding talk. Even a heart-felt testimony can distract your listeners from the message of your talk when it is too long or includes topics far adrift from your subject. Instead, your talk should flow naturally into your testimony. When concluding a talk, your testimony should be brief and reinforce the principles you spoke about.

Notice how Elder Richard G. Scott concludes his talk on prayer. His testimony is brief and relates directly to his topic:

> "**I testify** our Father will always answer your prayers in the way and in the time that will be for your best eternal good. In the name of Jesus Christ, amen."[74]

Elder Dallin H. Oaks beautifully demonstrates this as he concludes his talk about the two lines of communication with the Lord:

74 Using the Supernal Gift of Prayer, Richard G. Scott, April 2007 Conference

> "The children of God need both lines to achieve their eternal destiny. The restored gospel teaches both, and the restored Church provides both. **I testify** of the Lord's prophet, President Thomas S. Monson, who holds the keys that govern the priesthood line. **I testify** of the Lord Jesus Christ, whose church this is. And **I testify** of the restored gospel, whose truth can be known by each of us through the precious personal line to our Heavenly Father. In the name of Jesus Christ, amen."[75]

Watch as President Henry B. Eyring concludes his talk about trusting in God and His prophets with a challenge and then a testimony specific to the topic he discussed:

> "**If you** then go and do what He would have you do, your power to trust Him will grow, and in time you will be overwhelmed with gratitude to find that He has come to trust you. **I testify** that God speaks today through His chosen servants in The Church of Jesus Christ of Latter-day Saints. Thomas S. Monson is God's prophet. Our Heavenly Father and His Son, Jesus Christ, live and love us. **I so testify** in the name of Jesus Christ, amen."[76]

Finally, listen to Elder Bednar's moving testimony following his talk about the Holy Ghost. Again, notice that the testimony is brief and specific to the subject.

---

75 Two Lines of Communication, Dallin H. Oaks, Nov 2010 Conference

76 Trust in God, Then Go and Do, Henry B. Eyring, Nov 2010 Conference

> "**I bear witness** of the living reality of the Father and the Son. I testify the Holy Ghost is a revelator, a comforter, and the ultimate teacher from whom we should learn. And **I witness** that the blessings and gifts of the Spirit operate in the restored, in the true, and in the living Church of Jesus Christ in these latter days. **I so testify** in the sacred name of the Lord Jesus Christ, amen."[77]

Use Both Testimony and Call to Action

In many cases, an expression of testimony and a Call to Action are skillfully woven together into a masterful concluding statement. Look at how three different apostles use both in these powerful concluding statements:

> "**I bear** my special witness that [the Father and the Son] live. **When we** exercise our agency in righteousness, we come to know Them, become more like Them, and prepare ourselves for that day when 'every knee shall bow, and every tongue confess' that Jesus is our Savior. **May we** continue to follow Him and our Eternal Father, as we did in the beginning, **I pray** in the name of Jesus Christ, amen."[78]

> "**I know** the Lord can and will free the addicted from their bondage, for as the Apostle Paul proclaimed, 'I can do all things through Christ which strengtheneth me.' **I pray**, my brothers and sisters, that this may be so with those who may be struggling with this challenge at this time in their lives, and do so humbly in the name of Jesus Christ, amen."[79]

77 Receive the Holy Ghost, David A. Bednar, Nov 2010 Conference
78 Agency: Essential to the Plan of Life, Robert D. Hales, Oct 2010 Conference
79 O That Cunning Plan of the Evil One, M. Russell Ballard, Oct 2010 Conference

> "**May we** all recognize and give thanks for the incomparable gift of life we each enjoy and for the breath that He lends us daily. **May we** choose to have conviction at the crossroads of life and exercise faith in Jesus Christ. **My prayer is** that we will live by faith and not by fear. **I bear my witness** of God, who is our Heavenly Father, and His Son, Jesus Christ, who atoned for our sins, in the name of Jesus Christ, amen."[80]

We have learned that our conclusion can include both a brief testimony of the truths we discussed and a Call to Action which challenges the Saints to apply the principles in their lives. I encourage you to use both in your talks. As you study the examples above, you will have plenty of ideas to help close your talk in a way that gives the Holy Ghost a wonderful opportunity to testify to the principles while inspiring your listeners to put them into practice.

80 Live by Faith and Not by Fear, Quentin L. Cook, Oct 2007 Conference

Part II: Bearing Testimony in a Fast and Testimony Meeting

Members of the Church have the opportunity on the first Sunday of each month in fast and testimony meeting to share their testimonies with the Saints. The Brethren have stressed over and over that this opportunity is for bearing a brief, humble testimony about the principle doctrines of the gospel. It is not a time to teach the gospel, or thank people in the ward for fixing your fence, or tell about your recent vacation, or brag about your grandchildren. I've had bishops tell me that they worry more about fast and testimony meetings than any other in the Church because they never know when someone will get off track and detract from the spirit of the meeting.

Elder Dallin H. Oaks put it pretty bluntly:

> "A testimony of the gospel is not a travelogue, a health log, or an expression of love for family members. It is not a sermon. President Kimball taught that the moment we begin preaching to others, our testimony is ended... In all of our testifying we must avoid arrogance and pride."[81]

So, what is appropriate?

There are two principle purposes for bearing our testimony in a setting such as fast and testimony meeting. First, our testimonies become stronger as we bear them. When we share our testimony, the Holy Ghost bears witness in our

81 Testimony, Dallin H. Oaks, April 2008 Conference

hearts that the things we are saying are true. Second, members of the congregation have a similar experience as the Holy Ghost testifies to them of the truthfulness of our witness.

The Holy Ghost has the responsibility to bear witness to the truthfulness of the doctrines and principles of the gospel. Imagine that he is sitting, unseen, by an individual in the congregation who is in need of spiritual strength. As you stand up to bear your testimony, the Spirit waits for an opportunity to testify to this person's heart that your witness is true.

You stand up and begin…

> "I'd like to bear my testimony; I love my family and friends in the ward…"

The Holy Ghost is ready and waiting to testify to the truthfulness of the gospel.

> "…I'm thankful to our wonderful Sunday School teachers who do such a great job. I know that they spend a lot of time preparing their lessons and we should all do a better job at listening and applying what they teach us…"

The Spirit is still waiting, nothing yet to testify about.

> "…Last week was a difficult week in our family with John losing his job, but we feel of your faith and prayers. The bishopric and Relief Society have been so supportive. I want to thank the Lord for all the blessings He has given to me, in the name of Jesus Christ, Amen."

This was a touching and sincere declaration of gratitude, but there was no testimony given. It's true that some gospel principles were alluded to, such as service and prayer, but the fact is that the Holy Ghost had little opportunity to testify of the truthfulness of your testimony.

Let's look, in contrast, at a testimony given by Elder Oaks as an example of an appropriate message for a fast and testimony meeting. Notice how many opportunities the Spirit has to testify to our souls that the principle or doctrine is true:

> "I know that we have a Heavenly Father, whose plan brings us to earth and provides the conditions and destiny of our eternal journey. I know that we have a Savior, Jesus Christ, whose teachings define the plan and whose Atonement gives the assurance of immortality and the opportunity for eternal life. I know that the Father and the Son appeared to the Prophet Joseph Smith to restore the fullness of the gospel in these latter days. And I know that we are led today by a prophet, President Thomas S. Monson, who holds the keys to authorize priesthood holders to perform the ordinances prescribed for our progress toward eternal life. In the name of Jesus Christ, amen."[82]

When you bear your testimony, you can bear a general testimony of the basic doctrines of the Church (as Elder Oaks did above), or you can select a specific doctrine or principle that is particularly moving to you at this time.

82Testimony, by Dallin H. Oaks, April 2008 Conference

A testimony is a personal declaration of what you believe and why you believe it. If you have a brief experience or story that explains why you can testify of the truthfulness of a principle, it is appropriate to share it.

Watch as Alma does this as a part of his testimony:

> "Behold, I testify unto you that I do know that these things whereof I have spoken are true. And how do ye suppose that I know of their surety? Behold, I say unto you they are made known unto me by the Holy Spirit of God. Behold, I have fasted and prayed many days that I might know these things of myself. And now I do know of myself that they are true; for the Lord God hath made them manifest unto me by his Holy Spirit; and this is the spirit of revelation which is in me."[83]

If you have a faith-promoting story that illustrates your testimony, I encourage you to practice and polish it using the principles we talked about in Chapter Seven on stories before sharing it in testimony meeting. This helps you to be clear, accurate, and concise as you relate the experience.

Some might feel that if you practice parts of your testimony in advance—if it's not spontaneous and unrehearsed—it's less sincere. I beg to differ. Anything worth saying is worth saying well. We've all been in meetings where people start into a long, rambling rendition of a story that gets so off track, they completely forgot the point of their testimony. The more clearly and crisply you can relate your testimony, the better it will be.

83 Alma 5:45-6

Chapter 8
Overcoming Your Fear of Speaking

A 2001 Gallup Poll revealed that fear of public speaking is the #2 most distressing fear for Americans—second only to fear of snakes![84] According to the poll, most people would rather walk on a high ledge, handle spiders, or even go to the doctor and get a shot than stand up and speak to a group. If you get nervous at the thought of speaking in church, you're not alone. As you learned from my story in the introduction, I have been as afraid as anyone. In this chapter, you'll learn how to face this fear head-on and chop it down to a manageable level.

What Are We Afraid Of?

In order to tame this monster, it's a good idea to find out what it looks like. Here are a few of the top things we might be afraid of when speaking in church:

- looking silly
- mind going blank
- collapsing from fright
- sweating

84 http://www.gallup.com/poll/1891/Snakes-Top-List-Americans-Fears.aspx

- being less than perfect
- putting people to sleep
- voice squeaking
- shaking
- getting sick
- acting stupid
- tripping on the way to pulpit
- running out of things to say
- dropping dead
- people laughing at me
- fainting
- being boring
- putting people to sleep
- humiliation
- freezing up
- not as good as other speakers
- becoming emotional (crying)

As we look over the list, some are legitimate concerns, and others are pretty farfetched. But the most important fear is not even listed. We are afraid of being afraid. We worry that the anxiety of the moment will be painful and unpleasant. It's not speaking that is the enemy—it's fear. One thing I have learned over the years is that fear is real. Sometimes people will dismiss it by saying, "It's only in your mind." The truth is: fear can cause real physical symptoms, and is the major cause of procrastination and inactivity. It robs you of productivity and opportunity. In short, fear really is a monster that can have a huge, negative effect on your life.

We will tackle two kinds of fear in this book. The first is the fear, worry, and anxiety that occur before you give your talk. We'll consider these in this chapter. Second is the fear that occurs as you are delivering your talk. That will be dealt with in the next chapter.

Let's look at ten ways to stop fear in its tracks.

Get Perspective

Most fear is the result of how we have allowed our mind to view potential events in our lives. If we can change our mental perspective and view events through more objective eyes, the fear is lessened.

Refuse to worry about things that *might* happen. Have you ever stewed and fretted about something and then, when it happened, it wasn't nearly as bad as you thought it would be? The truth is that most of the things we worry about never happen. We may have spent months, even years, worrying about something, wasting time and mental energy, all the time slowly developing ulcers and other health problems, only to discover too late, when it actually happened, that there was no reason to worry after all. Give yourself a mental break and refuse to worry about things that might happen.

Also remember that most people are fearful about speaking, so you're in good company. You're not crazy or abnormal if you have a little anxiety about speaking. Others are able to face their fears and speak in church, and so can you. Members of the ward are your friends. They're pulling for you.

Finally, define your worries. As long as you have a general feeling of anxiety about an upcoming talk, it will continue to be a destructive monster. But when you expose your fears to the light of reason, they are much easier to deal with. It's often useful to ask yourself, "What is the worst thing that could happen?" Then, think through how you would handle it if it actually did. In most cases, once you identify the specific fear and decide how to handle it, the anxiety dissipates. For example, if your biggest worry is that you'll be boring and put people to sleep, you'll want to plan, polish, and practice some great stories that illustrate your points. (Review Chapter Six to learn how to do this.) Once you know that your talk is entertaining as well as educational, the fear of being boring is replaced by excitement to share your material. And your fear is gone.

Breathe

Fear and nervousness create anxiety, which can cause physical symptoms such as a racing heart beat or excessive perspiration. It's also emotionally painful. A great way to counteract these symptoms is calm, deep breathing. You can actually change the speed of your heart rate or lower your blood pressure by changing your breathing from shallow, quick breaths to steady, deep breathing. Try this: take your blood pressure when you are nervous or stressed. Then, sit quietly, breathe deeply for a moment, and take it again. One minute of calm breathing can be enough to stabilize your blood pressure and heart rate into the normal range. On the other hand, if you are sitting calmly at a heart rate of 70, you can raise it to 100+ simply by taking short, fast breaths for about thirty seconds.

Deep breathing, accompanied by calm, positive thoughts, can do wonders to alleviate fear and anxiety.

Mental Imaging / Visualization

Imagine you are with friends and family doing something fun, going out to dinner, playing games, watching a ball game, etc. Visualize how you would look, feel, and act. Are you composed, natural looking, smiling, relaxed, focusing on others instead of self? Now, take that image and project it into a speaking situation.

Imagine standing up to the pulpit, calm, composed, and prepared. You're smiling, relaxed, and friendly; you feel natural. You're excited about your material and focused on presenting it in the best way possible so your listeners can get your message. Hold this image in your mind as you practice and rehearse your talk. Visualize yourself standing up and delivering a dynamic, successful talk. The more real this mental image is, the more likely it is to become reality.

Too often, we do the opposite. We imagine all the things that could go wrong and then replay these distressing images over and over—and they haven't even happened! Train yourself to only visualize successful, positive mental images.

Talk to Yourself

We talk to ourselves every waking minute. Just like a computer, our minds constantly evaluate what is going on and anticipate the future. We tell our computer mind how to think and feel by the input we give it as we talk to ourselves. If we wake up saying, "It's going to be a bad day," and we continue to review that thought over and over all day long, guess what? It will be a bad day, no matter how many good things happen. If, on the other hand, you tell yourself over and over it will be a great day, and you believe it, it will be.

Let's relate this to speaking in church. What do you think will happen if you constantly feed your mind with statements like the following?

"I'm a terrible speaker."

"I always feel sick and sweat a lot when I get up in front of a group."

"I know I'll run out of things to say and look stupid."

"I hate speaking in church."

"I'll never think of anything clever to say."

"I'll probably trip on my words and everyone will laugh."

If you talk to yourself that way, you'll get more and more worried and anxious, and you might not do so well when you get up to speak.

If you choose positive affirmations instead, things will be much better. Replace the above thoughts with something like the following:

"I'm a great speaker."

"I'm excited to get up and share my message."

"I have plenty of great things to say—it'll be fun."

"I like speaking in church."

"I'll come up with some great points and interesting stories."

"I'll deliver my talk with poise and enthusiasm."

Picture someone you love and respect coming to you, fearful and worried about giving a talk in church. What would you say to build up and encourage them? You might say, "You're a great speaker, and everyone will love it" or "Don't worry, you have some amazing things to say." Why not give the same advice to yourself?

Constantly feed your mind with these positive thoughts to counteract negative thinking. Commit to only allowing thoughts that will build you up and help you give a great talk. When negative thoughts creep in, just reply with, "That won't happen," and immediately replace them with positive thoughts.

My friend, media personality Dian Thomas, said that she used to get nervous all the time before appearing on TV or giving a speech to a large group. Finally, she learned to say to herself, "Are you here to be nervous or to give a talk?" In this way, she was able to snap herself out of the worry and fear.

If you find you're getting anxious, just give yourself a little pep talk. Tell yourself how amazing your talk will be and that you are working hard to plan, prepare, and practice so it will be exceptional. Give yourself a little commercial on you. Tell yourself all the reasons why your message is important and remind yourself that you are giving your best effort to prepare and present a great talk. Assure yourself that you should be looking forward to your talk with enthusiastic anticipation.

Get Started

When we are fearful or anxious, we tend to procrastinate. We wait to get started to put off the agony. It's normal. Why do we do this? When we have an impending deadline, our minds feel the need to be working on it. When we worry, we can actually fool our minds into thinking we are working on the problem. Instead, it only gets worse. The more you put things off, the more intense your anxiety will be until it eventually either forces you to get started or you have a panic attack.

The minute you start, your anxiety and fear are replaced by action. Here is a cardinal rule:

Action destroys fear.

A common fear about talking in church is, "What will I say?" The more you worry about this, the bigger it gets, until all you can think about is worrying that you'll have nothing to say.

But once you actually get started (look at Chapter Three for easy, practical ideas), your mind will be flooded with potential ideas on what you could say. Your thoughts move from constantly worrying to coming up with ideas and solutions. As you ponder and focus, you give the Holy Ghost the opportunity to inspire you with additional thoughts. Pretty soon, you will have so many possibilities that this worry slinks away and dies.

Focus energy on planning, preparing, and practicing your talk. Put off worrying until you have prepared an excellent talk. By then, there will be little reason to worry.

If you want to permanently destroy fear, take action and get started. The more often you do, the easier it will be next time.

Be Prepared

For me, the biggest cause of worry is not being prepared. This is why we spent so much time in Chapters Three through Seven to help you plan, prepare, and practice your talk. If you have prepared well, the rest is easy. You have earned the right to relax.

I love the Lord's council to the Prophet Joseph Smith in 1831. Said He:

If ye are prepared ye shall not fear.[85]

85 D&C 38:30

You can:

- Prepare spiritually so that you can expect the Lord's help through the Holy Ghost
- Prepare and polish great content so you have plenty of good material
- Organize it into a structure that is easy to learn and adapt
- Practice and rehearse so you know you can do it well

Practice and Rehearse

Occasionally, I will talk with people who avoid preparing or rehearsing their talk by saying, "I'm at my best when I'm winging it" or "I do better when I shoot from the hip." Not true! You are at your best when you are prepared, polished, and practiced.

Perhaps some people feel that "winging it" works for them because once they actually stand up and start speaking, the fear evaporates. What they don't realize is that this is true for everyone, whether they have practiced or not. Either way, the anxiety is finally over. Unfortunately, the one who failed to prepare has had to live with anxiety for weeks, while the one who has prepared and practiced will give a much better talk and has experienced much lower levels of anxiety.

The key to confidence is practice, practice, practice. Speakers who make it look so simple, and so natural, are also the most practiced.

1. Practice whenever and wherever you can: in front of a mirror, in your car while driving, in the shower, or on a walk.
2. Practice breathing and smiling.
3. Practice your talk with a friend or small group. Practice looking in their eyes.
4. Practice your opening and your stories twice as much as the other parts of your talk.

Get Excited

The better your material, the more excitement and passion you have about it, the more excited you will be to share your message. This keeps your focus on the material rather than on how you are feeling. Nothing eliminates fear more than having something important to say that you are excited to share. Focus on the content, not on yourself.

Have a Strong Opening

As we have mentioned before, the time when you will tend to be the most nervous is right before your talk and just as you stand up. If you have a great opening that you know well and are excited to give, much of that fear goes away.

Follow the suggestions in Chapter Five to help you craft an interesting, dynamic opening. Practice so that you can give it without thinking. Then when you are sitting on the stand, instead of worrying, you can simply go over your opening in your mind and feel calm and confident.

Replace Fear with Faith

Did you ever wonder why there are so many references to wars in the Book of Mormon? These accounts help us know how we should fight our own personal battles in life. A common theme in these accounts is that those who turned to the Lord and trusted in Him were able to go into battle "in the strength of the Lord."[86] This means they were given greater strength, courage, assistance, and power to defeat any foe in their righteous cause. Those who did not trust in the Lord were referred to as being "weak."[87]

One such example is recorded in 3 Nephi, when the Nephites were gathered together in one place to make a stand against the Gadianton robbers who had overrun the land. When they attacked the Nephites, the robbers were a fearsome sight:

> "Behold, great and terrible was the day that they did come up to battle; and they were girded about after the manner of robbers; and they had a lamb-skin about their loins, and they were dyed in blood, and their heads were shorn, and they had head-plates upon them; and great and terrible was the appearance of the armies of Giddianhi, because of their armor, and because of their being dyed in blood.[88]

86 Mosiah 9:17
87 see Mormon 2:26
88 3 Nephi 4:7

Some people view speaking in church as a similarly terrifying spectacle. Let's see how the Nephites responded:

> "And it came to pass that the armies of the Nephites, when they saw the appearance of the army of Giddianhi, had all fallen to the earth, and did lift their cries to the Lord their God, that he would spare them and deliver them out of the hands of their enemies."[89]

Notice that they immediately turn to the Lord and pray for help. They put their trust in Him. Now, watch what happens. When the robbers see the Nephites praying, they are encouraged, thinking the Nephites have collapsed due to fear and terror. Not so:

> "But in this thing they were disappointed, *for the Nephites did not fear them*; but they did fear their God and did supplicate him for protection; therefore, when the armies of Giddianhi did rush upon them they were prepared to meet them; yea, *in the strength of the Lord* they did receive them."[90]

What removed the Nephite's fear? The same thing that will remove your fear and give you the strength and courage to stand up and speak with confidence—they trusted in the Lord. As a speaker in sacrament meeting, you are on His errand. You have a righteous purpose. If you will turn to him

89 3 Nephi 4:8
90 3 Nephi 4:10, emphasis added

with faith and trust, your fear will be taken away so that you can stand up and speak "in the strength of the Lord."

To those who preach the gospel (and speaking in church certainly counts) the Lord said:

> "I will go before your face. I will be on your right hand and on your left, and my Spirit shall be in your hearts, and mine angels round about you, to bear you up."[91]

The Lord will help you. Sacrament meeting is the most important meeting in the Church and it is very important to Heavenly Father. Certainly, He will bless and help you as you give it your best effort. Therefore, you have no reason to fear.

91 D&C 84:88

Chapter 9
Delivery—Giving Your Talk

Just as important as what you say is how you say it. We've all listened to talks that were written well, but didn't have much impact because the delivery lacked something.

Does Your Delivery Matter?

Does it really matter how well you deliver your talk? I think it does. Over and over in the scriptures, we are told of prophets who spoke with great power. No doubt they were blessed by the Spirit as they developed this skill, but I'm confident that they also had to work to develop the ability to speak with power. It is contrary to the economy of heaven for the Lord to bless us with skills until we put forth some effort. Once we do, He magnifies our abilities.

An example of this is Nephi and Lehi (sons of Helaman) who preached throughout the land of Nephi and then went to the Lamanites. The Lord blessed them to "preach with great power . . . therefore they did speak unto the great astonishment of the Lamanites."[92]

92 Helaman 5:17-19

You Can Speak with Power

You, too, can develop the skill of speaking with power. The first step is to have the Spirit of the Lord with you. This means striving to live worthy of, and praying for, the Spirit as you prepare and deliver your talk.

Second, you need to practice and work, striving to follow the principles in this chapter. As you do, the Lord will bless you to make up for any shortcomings that you might have—and send His Spirit to accompany your talk. Your best effort, combined with the blessings of the Lord, will yield dynamic results.

The important principle in this chapter is this:

> How *you deliver your talk can be just as important as* what *you say.*

Your presentation skills can be the difference between a talk that is easily forgotten and one that gets the message through to affect the lives of your listeners. Dynamics create energy, which holds your listener's attention.

The following suggestions can significantly improve the way you deliver your talk. Practice and adapt them, a little at a time, until they become a natural part of you.

If you are reading this book in order to prepare one talk, and you hope you'll never have to talk in church again (good luck with that), just focus on the first three suggestions: be yourself, look up, and speak up. These will make the biggest difference in your presentation.

If you speak on a regular basis, work on all the ideas, a few at a time, so you can slowly become better and better. Don't get so hung up on trying to implement everything at once that you become distracted and can't give your talk. It's more important to be present with your audience and focus on the content of your message than to stumble trying to implement too many delivery techniques at once.

When my daughter was fifteen, she joined the high school basketball team. She had been a pretty good player before, but she decided she wanted to improve. She worked hard at practice, and in her spare time began working with her grandfather, who had been an All-State player in high school and has since helped coach numerous players.

One day, she came home complaining, "My shot is totally messed up with these new techniques! I used to be able to make shots, but now I'm not making any. I'm having to learn to shoot all over again."

Despite her frustration, she kept practicing and working. Eventually, she was able to master the improved shooting techniques and enjoy a much higher percentage of made shots than she ever had before.

How does this apply to speaking? You might try some of the techniques below and feel a little silly, unnatural, or even distracted at first. Don't worry—just keep practicing and applying these ideas until they become natural and easy.

Be Yourself

The most important presentation tip I can give you is to be yourself. You might be thinking, "Who else would I be?" Unfortunately, when we get up in front of a group, we sometimes become a different person. Here's why.

Your brain sees a sea of heads on one side vs. only you on the other side, and calculates the odds of survival in a struggle. Let's face it—the odds are not too good. This triggers the brain to initiate the "fight or flight" reaction in your body. Blood moves away from your brain and your digestive system and into the muscles (so you can make a quick get-away if necessary). Adrenaline is released into your body, which increases your heart rate and dilates your blood vessels and airway passages. Although this can sharpen your reflexes and increase your energy, these changes can also cause many of the undesirable physical symptoms that some experience when they stand up in front of a group, such as shaking, perspiring, constricted voice, dry mouth, frozen facial muscles, and forgetting what you were going to say. These physical changes can make you appear to be an entirely different person.

In addition, when speakers get nervous, either they start talking very fast with no pauses and shallow breathing, or their voice becomes flat and expressionless—kind of like Winnie the Pooh's friend Eeyore. Whether you get fast or flat, neither of these styles is the real you.

Finally, although your listeners expect you to look and act natural, they also expect talks to be polished, forceful, and dynamic, even a little larger than life, so we sometimes try to be "superhero speaker" rather than ourselves.

As you can see, being yourself is a tall order. When you add up all the physical and emotional changes, plus living up to your perceived expectations of your listeners, being your normal, natural self is actually neither normal nor natural. Good public speaking only appears natural. In reality, it takes work, effort, and practice.

There are a lot of things you can do to reduce the impact of these physical and emotional pressures. If you will practice and rehearse the techniques in this chapter, plus pray for some extra help, you will soon find that your anxiety dissipates and your listeners will be much more engaged in your talk. You might even discover that speaking is fun!

Make it your goal to come across as close to your natural self as possible. In order to accomplish this, you'll need to practice speaking normally by rehearsing the techniques below, in front of a mirror at first, then before a small group. Practice adding your normal inflections and enthusiasm back into your speech. If you are telling a story, for example, add some life and animation to it, as you would if you were sitting on the couch at home telling the story to your friends. Practice breathing deeply and mentally calming yourself. Most of all, don't try to be someone you're not. Just be yourself.

Look Up

The number one thing you can do to improve your delivery is to look up from your notes and speak directly to the people in the congregation.

Looking down all the time makes you seem insincere and lacking conviction in your message. It gives your listeners the impression that you don't care about them. Reading your talk is like speaking to someone through a wall. There is a barrier. But if you look up and speak directly to your listeners, even if you occasionally refer to your notes, they will feel that you care about them and that you are speaking to them personally.

"If I look up from my notes," you might reply, "I won't know what to say!" Perhaps in the past this was true, but now that you have the tools you've discovered in this book—now that you know how to develop a structure that is easy to visualize and use; now that you know how to discover and polish your own unique stories; and now that you know how to practice and rehearse your talk—you should be able to give most of your talk without referring to your notes.

When you look up, instead of looking over their heads or letting your eyes wander back and forth across the congregation, try looking people in the eye, one at a time. This will help you in three ways.

First, it helps you connect with your listeners. Imagine going to a party where you meet new people one at a time, but instead of looking at them when you are introduced, you look over their heads, or let your eyes wander all over the room. You obviously wouldn't establish a very personal connection with the people you meet. Speaking to a group of people you don't know is like meeting people one at a time. You need to look them in the eye and talk to them individually. Try holding their gaze for a few seconds so they feel like you're interested in them as an individual.

If you're giving your talk in your home ward where you know almost everyone, you have the added advantage of familiarity, but the principle is the same. As you give your talk, practice looking at one person at a time, as if you are greeting them in the hall or on a neighborhood street corner. Speak to them directly for a few seconds, then greet someone else with your eyes and speak to them. Speaking coach J. Douglas Jefferys puts it like this: "You are not talking to a group of individuals—you are talking to individuals in a group."[93]

Eye contact is just as important to getting your message across as the words you say. Try this: next time you go to a movie or watch a show on TV, notice how much you look at the eyes of the actors. We actually look at the eyes more than anything else such as costumes, hands, mouth, etc. As you pay attention, you'll also discover that much of the meaning in the words the actors say comes from what they do with their eyes. Good actors can convey volumes of meaning by the way they move their eyes. For example, if you say, "That's great!" and roll your eyes while you're saying it, we understand that you are being sarcastic. On the other hand, if you look someone in the eye with intensity as you say the same words, they carry a totally different meaning.

93 90 Minutes to Killer Presentation Skills, DVD Training Program by J. Douglas Jefferys

Eye contact also helps you add the element of trust. You've heard people say, "I didn't trust that guy—he wouldn't look me in the eye." On the few occasions when I have been privileged to meet a General Authority or hear them talk in person, they always look you right in the eye. It almost seems like they are looking through you and perhaps, through the Spirit, they are. When you look the members of your congregation in the eye, they will feel that you are confident, credible, and trustworthy. They will feel that you, like the Apostle Paul, can declare: "I am not ashamed of the gospel of Christ…"[94]

Eye contact also helps you with the "fight or flight" reaction we spoke about earlier. If you can train yourself to focus on only one person at a time, it dramatically reduces the mental playing field. Your conversation is now one-on-one rather than one vs. a hundred. There is less of a stimulus for the distressing physical and emotional symptoms we discussed earlier.

Ask any truly great speaker how many people they have spoken to at a time. They will invariably say, "One!" They may have spoken before crowds of hundreds, even thousands, of people, but they always speak to one person at a time. This keeps the speech personal and intimate, no matter how many people are in the audience.

This is something you'll want to practice with your friends. Perhaps you could sit around a table with your friends and try looking them in the eye, one at a time, while you give your talk. Try holding each person's gaze for a complete sentence or thought. Then look at someone else.

94 Romans 1:16, see also 2 Corinthians 7:14

Pay particular attention to this principle as you open your talk. Some professional speakers look over the audience and choose in advance the one person to whom they will give their opening statement. When you're sitting on the stand waiting to give your talk, you might do the same. I'd encourage you to select someone who is warm and accepting, someone whom you would feel comfortable talking with in the hall.

Speak Up

Have you ever listened to a talk where the speaker was so quiet you could hardly hear? How was it? Chances are, you don't remember very much about it—other than the fact that you couldn't hear what they were saying.

Sometimes, members feel that they should speak quietly as a sign of reverence. But in doing so, they may actually be sending the wrong message. When you speak softly, people tend to think that you lack confidence or that you are unsure about what you're saying.

Show that you have conviction in what you are saying. Speak up! Make sure that everyone in the ward can hear your talk. Here again, our rule is paramount.

It doesn't matter what you say, it matters what gets through.

Remember our tripod of intellectual, spiritual, and emotional communication? If the members of the congregation have to strain to catch your meaning, if they are only able to catch two-thirds of your talk because your voice is hard to hear, how much emotional or spiritual communication can take place? Not much.

I encourage you to speak up. Pretend there is no microphone and you need to project your voice all the way to the back of the room.

Some people are intimidated by the microphone. When they start speaking and hear their voice coming through the speakers in the ceiling, it makes them nervous. So, they speak more and more softly, until, pretty soon, no one can hear them at all. Don't worry about the microphone. Just look people in the eye and speak loud enough so they can hear every word, inflection, and emotion in your voice.

Speed

As we discussed earlier, when people get nervous, it tends to interrupt their normal speaking speed. They get fast or flat. Either way, it makes your talk hard to understand. If you tend to fall into this pattern, follow these tips:

1. Practice speaking at normal speed in front of a friend or even a small group. Have them tell you if you are too fast or slow.
2. Take a deep breath to calm yourself before beginning. Continue breathing deeply throughout your talk.
3. Know your opening so well that you can give it with out thinking. That gives you a chance to focus on your delivery. If you can establish a good rhythm in the opening, the rest of your talk will tend to continue with it.

4. Vary your speed to illustrate your message. Pause on important words, and speed up in other areas. When it comes to the speed of your talk, the enemy is sameness.

Variety

Imagine how boring a concert or symphony would be if they played the same note, over and over, with the same tempo and volume. A hallmark of great music is variety. Some moments are fast, others are slow. Tempo, volume, tone, pitch, mood, key—something is always changing. It makes the music exciting and interesting. It skillfully reflects our moods and emotions. Great speakers are the same. Some moments are fast and others are slow. You might experience loud and soft, happy and sad, funny and serious—all in the same talk. Great speeches, like great music, are characterized by variety.

Just as the dynamics of music affect the mood, so your speaking dynamics should naturally support what you are trying to say. If you are telling a story about something that was quick or exciting, pick up the tempo and volume of your speech. When you have an important point to make, you should slow down and articulate your words. Variety in inflection, dynamics, and expression can be used to emphasize and illustrate the different parts of your talk.

Did you know that you can change the meaning of any sentence by the inflection you put on your voice? Try this. Read the following sentence out loud:

I did not see him throw the ball.

Now read it again aloud, each time putting a dynamic stress on the bolded word, followed by a short pause as shown below. Notice how the meaning and tone of the sentence changes each time.

- ***I*** did not see him throw the ball. (Someone else saw it, not me.)
- I ***did not*** see him throw the ball. (Emphatic denial)
- I did not ***see*** him throw the ball. (I'm sure he threw it, I just didn't see him do it.)
- I did not see ***him*** throw the ball. (I saw someone else throw it.)
- I did not see him ***throw*** the ball. (He didn't throw it, he kicked it.)
- I did not see him throw the ***ball.*** (It was the bat I saw him throw.)

After this exercise, can you doubt the importance of voice inflection? Practice giving emphasis to specific words or phrases in your talk so your meaning is crystal clear.

When I was in the MTC, one of my teachers was Brother Brockbank. He was fun, dynamic, and full of enthusiasm as he helped us to learn what we needed to know. However, once in a while, if he had something important or profound to say, he would squat down on his haunches, look each of us directly in the eye and speak very slowly and clearly, then pause. In this way, he emphasized the message so no one would miss it. While I don't encourage you to squat down when you're speaking in church, you can emphasize an important point by following Brother Brockbank's example: look people in the eye and speak slowly and clearly, then pause to emphasize your point. Notice that the emphasis was caused not just by what he did, but how it contrasted from his normal cadence, which was quick and enthusiastic. If your normal speech is slow and quiet, you won't add much emphasis by speaking more slowly and quietly. On the contrary, you'll likely lull your listeners to sleep. The emphasis is in the variety.

Have you ever sat around a campfire and stared into the flames? I can do it for hours. It is captivating, even mesmerizing. Why? Because it is always changing—the flames continuously vary in size, intensity, shape, and color. They are in constant motion. There is endless variety. This captures and keeps our attention. When you add variety to your delivery by constantly changing your speed, tone, volume, and mood, your talks can be just as captivating.

Pauses

Pausing gives members of the congregation a chance to process what you said. Here is an important principle:

People don't start listening until you stop talking.

Have you ever been in a sacrament meeting where the speaker became emotional and paused for an extended period? Notice how it adds emphasis to what was said just before they paused and how we listen even more intently, waiting for them to recover.

If you plow through your talk, seldom giving your listeners a chance to internalize or think about what you say, they will get much less out of your message. Listening to a speaker who does not pause once in a while is like reading a book with no pictures, graphics, or even paragraphs to add a little variety. When you pause between ideas, your listeners are better able to mentally absorb your previous statement and are ready to listen to another.

On this topic, Mark Twain once said, "The right word may be effective, but no word was ever as effective as a rightly timed pause."[95]

These don't have to be dramatic, long pauses and they should not seem unnatural. The best place to pause is when you:

1. Are transitioning from one idea to another
2. Take a deep breath
3. Glance at your notes
4. Change eye contact from one person to another

Pausing at the right moment, for the right amount of time, is a skill you will develop as you practice and observe the reaction of the congregation.

95 http://www.brainyquote.com/quotes/quotes/m/marktwain124428.html

New speakers are often uncomfortable with even a brief silence, thinking it's their job to fill every second of space with their magnificent voice, but great speakers have learned the art of the pause. I encourage you to pay attention to your favorite speakers, whether they live in your own ward or you watch a broadcast of general conference. Notice the pauses. When do they pause, and for how long? Do the pauses seem natural or forced? How do you and other members of the audience react? How does it affect the meaning and impact of the message?

Enthusiasm

When I listen to a speaker, the first thing that hits me is their level of enthusiasm. Do they seem happy to be there? Are they excited about the topic and anxious to tell me how they feel about it? Public speaking expert Dale Carnegie was fond of saying: "Depth of conviction counts more than height of logic, and enthusiasm is worth more than knowledge."[96]

What does this word "enthusiasm" mean, anyway? The Greek derivation means "God in us." At its core, enthusiasm relates not only to our level of conviction and excitement, but also to our spiritual roots. Elder James E. Faust said, "A sacred light comes to our eyes and countenances when we have a personal bond with our loving Heavenly Father and His Son..."[97]

96 Stand And Deliver, Simon & Schuster Audio, Dale Carnegie Training, 2007 (This quote is originally attributed to David Peebles.)

97 The Light in Their Eyes, James E. Faust, Oct 2005 Conference

The Savior put it this way:

> "Ye are the light of the world. A city that is set on an hill cannot be hid. Neither do men light a candle, and put it under a bushel, but on a candlestick; and it giveth light unto all that are in the house. Let your light so shine before men…"[98]

I urge you to seek for this light and let your enthusiasm shine as you give your talk.

True communication, whether it's one-on-one or speaking to a group, is a transfer of feeling. Enthusiasm is contagious. If you have conviction and excitement about your topic and it shines forth through your presentation, your listeners will begin to feel enthusiastic about it as well.

David M. McConkie, first counselor in the Sunday School general presidency, once said:

> "Successful gospel teachers love the gospel. They are excited about it. And because they love their students, they want them to feel as they feel and to experience what they have experienced. To teach the gospel is to share your love of the gospel. Brothers and sisters, a teacher's attitude is not taught: it's caught."[99]

Posture and Body Language

When you stand up to give your talk, make sure that your body language and posture contribute to, rather than detract

98 Matthew 5:14-16
99 Gospel Learning and Teaching, David M. McConkie, Oct 2010 Conference

from, your message.

When at the pulpit, stand still. This demonstrates that you are firm and sure of what you want to stay. If you weave around, fidget, or rock back and forth, it gives the impression that you are nervous or unsure of your message.

Rest your hands on the pulpit (not in your pocket). It's okay to gesture to help you to get the message across, but only do it if it's natural for you. Avoid touching your face or fidgeting with your hair, clothes, etc. Finally, keep your hands open and relaxed. When we get nervous, we tend to make a fist, or grip the podium as if we're afraid we might fall to our death if we let go. But a relaxed, open hand puts our listeners (and us) at ease.

Most of all, adopt a calm, confident demeanor. If you're not feeling particularly confident, that's okay. Just act as if you did. Shakespeare gave us some great advice when he said, "Assume a virtue if you have it not."[100] In other words, if you want to feel confident, act confident. If you want to feel happy or enthusiastic, adopt the countenance of one who is. Pretty soon, your feelings will follow.

Breathe

Deep breathing helps you speak naturally, calms your nerves, and sends oxygen to your brain. It also helps you project your voice so your listeners can hear you.

Take a deep breath before standing and continue breathing deeply when you pause between thoughts. Practice

100 Hamlet, William Shakespeare, 3:4

breathing through your nose when possible so the audience doesn't perceive you as gulping for air.

Don't Exceed Your Time

Few things distract a congregation more than a speaker who keeps talking when their time is up.

"But," you say, "the previous speaker went way over and I only had five minutes to give my seventeen-minute talk!"

I know it's not fair to reduce your talk just to keep the meeting on time. But the reality is:

No one hears anything you say after the meeting is supposed to have ended.

This is not just true for a speaker in sacrament meeting, it also applies to Sunday school, priesthood, and Relief Society lessons. In our modern culture, people are keenly aware of time. They know when you should have finished, and when that time comes and goes, without you seeming to notice you should have quit 5 minutes ago, your listeners tend to get nervous and shift their focus from your message.

"Will I have to cut my Sunday School lesson short?" someone might be thinking. Children will pull on their parents' arms, saying, "When will this be over?" Some members might even get up and leave to get ready for their next class, distracting the congregation even more.

My advice to you—say "amen" when your time is up.

How do you cut down your talk to make it fit without

completely losing the thread of your talk? It's easy with the structure chart from Chapter Four. Just give your Opening and Anchor Statement. If there's time, choose one of your Points and give it, along with its accompanying Story and Application. If not, just move directly to the Summary and close with your Testimony and Call to Action.

In this way, you can still get your overall point across while staying within your time, the Spirit has a chance to testify of your message, and the congregation will love you, so they will be more likely to listen and internalize your message.

What about Props, Assistants, Entertainment, or Visual Aids?

The Brethren have directed that "Members should not use visual aids in sacrament meeting or stake conference. Such teaching methods are more appropriate in classroom settings and leadership meetings."[101] We should avoid distracting gestures, theatrics, sound effects, or any other activities that could detract from the sacred nature of sacrament meeting. Also, please don't embarrass or criticize people in your talk—even in fun—or share private information without their permission.

We should be careful not to overstep the bishop's authority to determine what happens in our meetings. If we have been given an assignment to speak for fifteen minutes, it means we are to speak for fifteen minutes. It does not mean that we have fifteen minutes to orchestrate whatever we want

101 Handbook 2, Administering the Church 18.4, 2010

to happen. The Church Handbook is clear that everything that occurs in our sacrament meetings is under the presiding direction of the bishopric.[102] Even though the person conducting may say, "We'll now turn the time over to..." they are not turning the actual direction of the meeting over to you for the duration of your talk. Therefore, you should not do anything that varies from your assignment, such as inviting a member of the congregation to come to the pulpit to assist you or to give a portion of your talk. Also, there is a place for sacred music in sacrament meetings, but it would be inappropriate to sing part of your talk, or even ask the congregation to sing, without prior approval. When in doubt, please talk to a member of the bishopric.

What to Do about Distractions

What should you do if something happens during your talk? What if a baby starts screaming or someone's cell phone rings?

In most cases, just continue on as if nothing has happened. One of the most amazing demonstrations of this was in general conference in April 1989. Elder Howard W. Hunter moved to the pulpit with a walker to give his talk. This was the first time in two years that he had been able to stand to give his talk, as he had been confined to a wheelchair. Mid-sentence, he suddenly lost his balance and fell over backwards, cracking a rib. Several of the Brethren immediately helped him up. Without skipping a beat, Elder Hunter continued with his

102 Handbook 2, Administering the Church 18.2.2, 2010

talk—just as if nothing had happened! Most people in the audience and on radio never knew that he had fallen.

If the distraction is so obvious or loud that you can't help but acknowledge it, simply pause until the distraction is over, then continue as if nothing happened. You may be tempted, due to nervousness or perhaps trying to lighten the mood, to make a spontaneous comment about the incident. Try to resist this impulse because it completely distracts your listeners away from your topic, and it's easy to make an impromptu comment you later wish you could retract. Just continue with your talk. This quickly turns the focus away from the distraction and back to the content of your message.

Be Genuine

Many years ago, a cute couple in our ward was asked to give a lesson in Sunday School. The family was from Argentina, and although their English was good, it was still a little shaky. They were obviously nervous and a bit self-conscious. As I came into the class, I noticed that sitting right behind me was a woman, not a member, who I knew was taking the missionary discussions. I admit that I was a little hesitant about whether she would have a good experience in the class.

The couple covered the topic simply, keeping to the manual for the most part and even reading sections of the lesson. Their speech was slow and a little halting, due to the language barrier. In other words, they violated many of the presentations tips we've discussed in this chapter.

But there was something about the way their simple words dripped with honesty and sincerity that took me aback. Many times they looked at each other and described how they had discussed the principles in the lesson together at home and with their children. Their faith and devotion to the gospel was readily evident in their manner and speech. As they bore testimony of the truthfulness of the gospel and the subject of the lesson, the Spirit was very strong. It was a wonderful, spiritual feast for me—and for the investigator.

My point is, the techniques in this chapter are important and they will improve your speaking skills so you can get your message across, but no amount of technique can make up for a lack of sincerity or a genuine desire to share your testimony of the principles of the gospel.

Delivery Tips in a Nutshell

1. Be yourself, work on appearing natural.
2. Look up from your notes and meet people in the eye.
3. Speak up so you can be heard.
4. Add variety to your speed, volume, and tone.
5. Speak with expression.
6. Pause to add emphasis and give your listeners a chance to absorb your message.
7. Infuse your talk with enthusiasm.
8. To feel confident, adopt the demeanor of a confident person.
9. Breathe deeply to stay calm and relaxed.
10. Stay within your time.

11. If there are distractions, pause briefly, then continue as normal.
12. Be sincere and genuine.
13. Arrive early.
14. When appropriate, get a drink of water before the meeting.
15. Smile and be upbeat.
16. Turn off your cell phone. Imagine how embarrassing and distracting it would be if your phone rang during your talk. Even the vibration can distract you.
17. When you use scriptures in your talk, don't ask members of the congregation to open their books and read along with you.[103]
18. Dress appropriately. The better you look, the more confident you will feel. Avoid clothes that are loud or extreme which could distract members from focusing on your message. "How we dress is an important indicator of our attitude and preparation for any activity in which we will engage."[104]
19. Speak clearly. Articulate your words. Don't mumble or trail off at the end of a sentence.
20. Keep your hands away from your face.
21. Avoid filler words such as "um, mmm, er, uh." The more you rehearse, the less likely you are to use these words.
22. Don't read your talk, tell it.
23. Don't apologize or deprecate yourself. Just be confident and do your best.
24. Use simple gestures to illustrate your thoughts.
25. Relax, have fun, and enjoy sharing your message.

---

103 Handbook 2, Administering the Church 18.2.2, 2010

104 Sacrament Meeting and the Sacrament, Dallin H. Oaks, Oct 2008 Conference

Chapter 10
PUTTING IT ALL TOGETHER

Congratulations! You've made it all the way through this book. You've learned the foundational principles of speaking in church as well as some practical, nuts-and-bolts ideas on how to design and deliver a great sacrament meeting talk. Now what?

If you have a speaking assignment coming up, I urge you to start now. Get out a notebook, turn back to Chapter Three, and start developing your content. Make a copy of the blank structure chart in the appendix and use the information in Chapter Four to sort through and reduce your content into an organized talk. Use Chapters Five through Seven for in-depth information about the three most important parts of your talk: the Opening, Stories, and your closing Testimony and Call to Action. Use the information in Chapters Eight and Nine to harness your fears and sharpen your speaking skills. Practice and rehearse your talk until you know it well. Then, stand up and give it.

If you'll follow these steps, I promise that you'll be a more confident, poised, polished, and effective speaker. Not only will you feel less nervous, but you will be excited to share your talk with the congregation. You'll discover that an opportunity to speak in church is something to look forward to, rather than avoid. It can even be fun.

Most importantly, you'll find that speaking is an opportunity to serve your fellow members—and the Lord. When we think of service, we tend to think of things like shoveling snow for a neighbor, bringing dinner to a sick friend, or visiting someone in the hospital. These are all wonderful, but think about this. Nothing is more beneficial to a struggling soul who comes to church looking for hope than words of encouragement, comfort, peace, and a renewal of faith and testimony.

Elder Jeffrey R. Holland put it quite succinctly:

> "Most people don't come to church looking merely for a few new gospel facts or to see old friends, though all of that is important. They come seeking a spiritual experience. They want peace. They want their faith fortified and their hope renewed. They want, in short, to be nourished by the good word of God, to be strengthened by the powers of heaven. Those of us who are called upon to speak or teach or lead have an obligation to help provide that, as best we possibly can."[105]

I personally can't think of a better act of sacrifice and service

105 A Teacher Come From God, Jeffrey R. Holland, May 1998 Conference

than the time you spend studying, praying, developing stories and examples, organizing, and practicing so you can deliver your message in the best possible way. Building faith and testimony—giving encouragement and joy—that is the pinnacle of service.

What better way to serve God and His Saints than by giving a great talk in church. I testify that as you apply and practice what you have learned, you can be the difference in someone's life. You can do it!

Appendix
STRUCTURE CHART

How to Use the Structure Chart

In this appendix, you will find a blank version of the Structure Chart, which you can duplicate and use for your talks. You can also download it at SpeakingInChurch.com. You can see the filled-in version of this chart on page 63.

The chart is explained in detail in Chapter Four. Simply plug in the appropriate pieces of content by writing key words and phrases in each shape to remind yourself of what you will say in each section of your talk. If you are using a scripture or General Authority quote, you can write it in the margin or on the back of your chart to make sure you quote it correctly.

Once you have practiced your talk a few times, this chart could be all that you need to take to the pulpit. Even if you take your other notes with you (for security-just in case) you will probably not need to refer to them. As long as you know what you want to say in each section, you have essentially learned your talk.

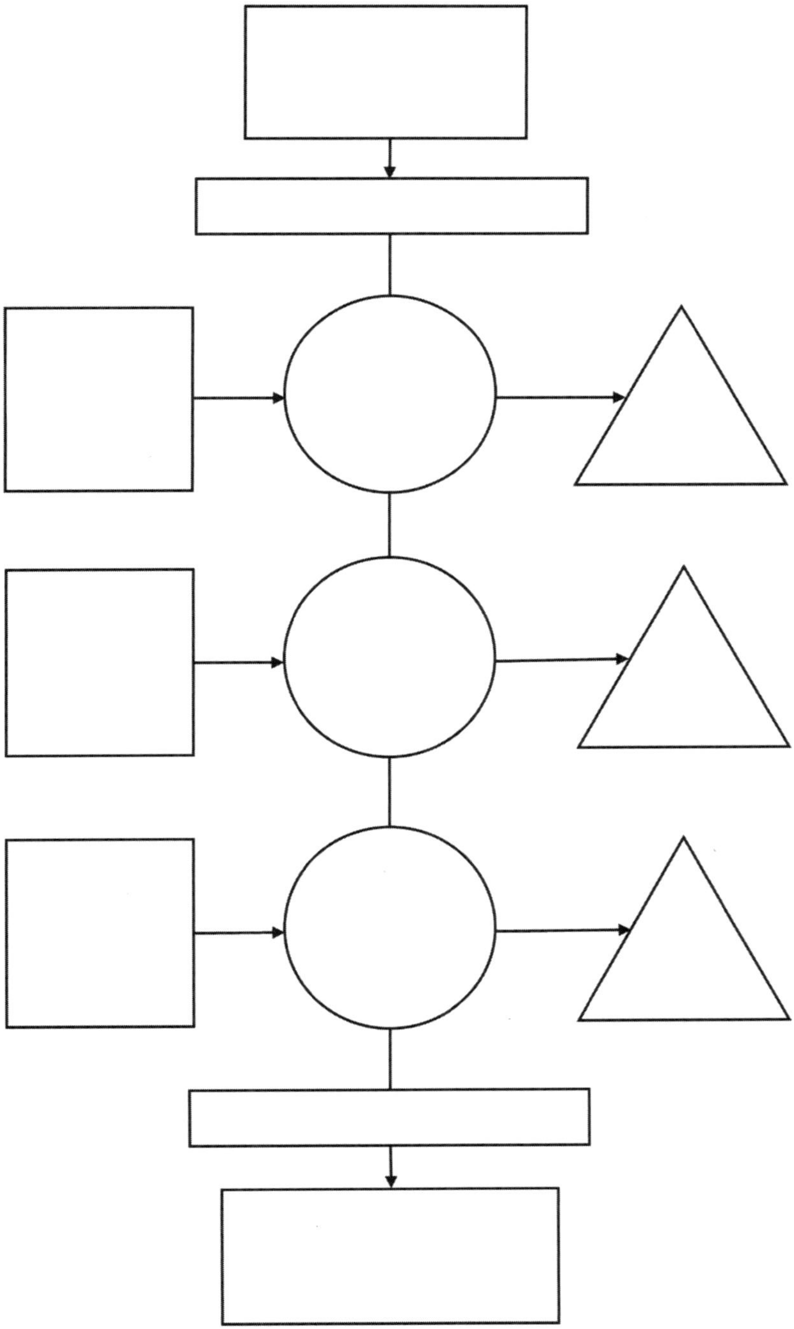

N

O

P

R

S

About the Author

Bill Mansell is a native of Utah and graduated from Brigham Young University with a degree in English. He is president of MindPerk, Inc., which specializes in business training and personal motivation products and services. He has consulted with thousands of companies and individuals worldwide, helping them to improve, motivate, and train their team members. Bill is a devoted member of The Church of Jesus Christ of Latter-day Saints and currently serves as a high councilor in his stake. He and his wife, Marquette, are the parents of three children.

www.SpeakingInChurch.com